T0077880

TO WARM THE SOLITARY NIGHT

—

A BOOK OF POEMS

DON EDWARDS

authorHOUSE®

AuthorHouse™
1663 Liberty Drive
Bloomington, IN 47403
www.authorhouse.com
Phone: 833-262-8899

© 2021 Don Edwards. All rights reserved.

No part of this book may be reproduced, stored in a retrieval system, or transmitted by any means without the written permission of the author.

Published by AuthorHouse 08/05/2021

ISBN: 978-1-6655-3360-7 (sc)
ISBN: 978-1-6655-3361-4 (hc)
ISBN: 978-1-6655-3359-1 (e)

Print information available on the last page.

Any people depicted in stock imagery provided by Getty Images are models, and such images are being used for illustrative purposes only. Certain stock imagery © Getty Images.

This book is printed on acid-free paper.

Because of the dynamic nature of the Internet, any web addresses or links contained in this book may have changed since publication and may no longer be valid. The views expressed in this work are solely those of the author and do not necessarily reflect the views of the publisher, and the publisher hereby disclaims any responsibility for them.

I had wanted such a love, like all the
writers of those rapturous ballads
So to warm the solitary night always.
And then suddenly you appeared with
your lips and with those eyes
While I was —

From "When You Gave Your Self"

VOLUME ONE

When You Gave Your Self

When you gave your self to me, it was the greatest gift you could have given.
With your beauty and grace, your brilliance the brightest star in heaven,
You made every moment a surprise.

I had wanted such a love, like all the writers of those rapturous ballads
So to warm the solitary night always.
And then suddenly you appeared with your lips and with those eyes
While I was —

Drinking beer and dancing to someone else's music,
Making love when the evening was through,
Falling further apart each succeeding twilight,
Listening quiet as our love faded into blue.

All I needed was to be there and to be gentle, to lose my self and take your
hand through the day
But I did not know how to sustain us, how to keep you in focus and not be
foolishly drawn away.
I could not hold steady with you as I should.

Such an open acceptance, such a tender warmth —
How you tickled my ear with your whisper,
It was your touch that created our world
While I was —

Drinking beer and dreaming to someone else's music,
Making love when the evening was through,
Falling further apart each succeeding session,
Listening quiet as our love faded into blue.

Losing faith as the result of a false direction,
Nothing was left to hold to as our own song died away.

My unmoored heart became only a reflection
Of what was prominent in each confusing day.

I had my own dream that floated high above us.
Sometimes it was all that I could see.
Your beauty was so close by
It seemed you would always be with me
While I was —

Drinking beer and dreaming to someone else's music,
Making love when the evening was through,
Falling further apart each succeeding session,
Listening quiet as our love faded into blue.

But then you announced that you were leaving
Lost among the many colored lights of my world
You just walked away — out of sight — disappeared
And my life has never been the same.

And that dream that still floats above
Has been no substitute for you.
And I still remember when
And long for what might have been
While I was —

Drinking beer and dreaming to someone else's music,
Making love when the evening was through,
Falling further apart each succeeding session,
Listening quiet as our love faded into blue.

The Skinny Kid

The skinny kid with the ratty backpack followed me in,
Eyes blazing hot and wildly unfocused, sour smelling and thin,
And asked for a cup of water at the In 'n' Out by the bus stop,
Mumbling low to no one at all as nobody was looking or cared.
His face the color of the dusty river bank, hungry too I guess,
And too weak to jerk the chained tip jar loose from the register,
He dashed empty-handed back out the door to his snarling home — the street.

This place where the sidewalks are lined with blue tarps, rusty bikes, and
shopping carts
Where the hunger of slouched figures is hidden by the drug
Where anguish like a tattered blanket covers all

This city of hunger
This city of street kids
This city of the lost
This city without angels

I should have known when he asked for a cup of water that he had no money.
I should have known that he was hungry and tired from the day
As the old man in front of him was busily focused
On ordering his own dinner and this was all that he could see
Living in another world because a dollar made the difference
Between the customer and the unwanted one now lost among the traffic.

This dream home where food is to be had for money
Where a roof requires steady supplies of cash
Where a salary will get you through the month
In a different world

This city of the limousine
This city of beautiful people
This city of warmth and sunshine
This city of angels

He who sleeps on the sidewalk on a roll of paper towels,
A jacket as his pillow, exposed to the traffic going by
To home or office with roofs and walls
Has no place to be secure, no one who will talk to him because if he is dirty
he must be bad.
He is a human disposed of and forgotten but who still gets hungry and lonely
and sad.
So many are now swimming with their noses just above the line.
So much is lost so quickly as they sink quiet beneath the brine.

No chance to grow or nurture
No chance to lounge in the shade
No way to eat without a dollar
No way to live with and unafraid

I Live In This City

I live in this city of hunger where losers can't survive
Within this city of street kids who won't get out alive
This city of the lost where so many lucky still thrive
This city of blind angels without the faith to help revive

This city of the limousine so sleek and silent borne
This city of beautiful people with lives so swift and numb
This city of warmth and sunshine where cold is overcome
This city of still born angels that has not learned yet to mourn

When we wake up in the daylight with our loved ones close beside
When we feed ourselves from the plenty which fills our pantries wide
When the soft glow of our locked up home shines upon our success
Then we should feel all these blessings and share with those in distress

When I Awoke

When I awoke, the bright sun's warmth made me tingle to the bone
I danced with my self, sang my song, and dreamed of not being alone.
Then came the vision of you — your smile and those magical eyes
And how you would want to be with me and make our love your prize

And we'd live out this dream of a life that would be made our own
Both loving and respectful as we walk toward our self made home
To create a joy and fulfillment to shelter from the hard stinging rain
While we kiss away the moments that would drag us through life's pain

Though it has not all been easy as we took on each day's task
We two have made a statement and given more than we have asked
Ours are the hearts that have grown together like roses above the thorns
Two souls as one entwined to bring joy and leave others to mourn

After all this time, the clock ticks on toward evening and I will soon again
be free
As the world spins toward its ending I will no longer need to be
As fate directs our movements as destiny guides our way
I need only smile take your hand and watch the dying of the day

I Carry It All

I carry it all upon my back — the burden of being upright
To push through the muck that resists all motion doing what must be done
To find the words that blend new found colors into the portrait of the world
To calm the storm, lower the tide, and make a path across the sea so bright.

Look at me. Look at me. Look at me.
I'm the one who's here for you.
Look at me. Look at me. Look at me.
Let's turn to the warmth of brown our now chilly home out in the blue.

Since this is my chance, then let me trace a rainbow across the sky.
Since this is my day, then I've got to be doing, so you may walk beside.
I pray for the wisdom to find the words that will float up above
Where they may bend gentle over all to make a better day for love.

Look at me. Look at me. Look at me.
I'm the one who's here for you.
Look at me. Look at me. Look at me.
Let's turn to the warmth of brown our now chilly home out in the blue.

I have not come to offer you the peace and joy of understanding
But have brought a sword to force you from the rut you have been demanding.
Deny yourself hope and comfort and you will find your way to replacing
The easy rest-filled journey of the ignorant and the complacent.

Look at me. Look at me. Look at me.
I'm the one who's here for you.
Look at me. Look at me. Look at me.
Let's turn to the warmth of brown our now chilly home out in the blue.

And here then we will find the home that has been waiting since before the
fall —
A new garden of doing and being without the curse of tomorrow
Where now is the answer to when we must respond to each and every call
And all of our thoughts and actions are aimed to create a world of less sorrow.

Look at me. Look at me. Look at me.
I'm the one who's here for you.
Look at me. Look at me. Look at me.
Let's turn to the warmth of brown our now chilly home out in the blue.

In Memoriam

The card read In Memoriam
A tragic rite where each line opens with "Remember when..."
Where memories are picked off like daisy petals one by one
And where the love recalled warms our selves once more as you have done.

Remember when I fell from the tree back first to the ground
Where I first knew the fright of sudden pain and being knocked down.
Dad, with your hands so big and strong you came right to my aid.
You picked me up, steadied me, and sent me on my way.

I remember all about you
How you were always there
How it was you would forever care
How everything could be repaired
I remember you.

Remember how sick I was that winter so fevered, pale and thin,
That time when the snow blew hard and the doctor wasn't in.
You nursed me back saving my worthless soul you man among the men
Who would fix what was wrong whatever it might have been.

I remember how you kept us warm in clothes and home and also fed.
You somehow put a roof over all our days and all our heads
And never asked for anything or shared the daily dreads
Of raising a family without a break or thanks ever being said.

I remember all about you
How you were always there
How it was you would forever care
How everything could be repaired
I remember you.

Remember the time years later when the police took me in
When they decided that with my look I must have been the one.
Remember how you bailed me out and had the lawyer to spin
A truthful tale that he sculpted from the jumpsuit of lies they had spun.

So here we are remembering when and how you lived your days,
How you gave us all direction throughout this tragic maze
And how we miss your sonorous voice and your strong yet gentle ways
And all the kindness and love you let us feel in your sure gaze.

I remember all about you
How you were always there
How it was you would forever care
How everything could be repaired
I remember you.

More than anything you did or would do, I remember you being there.
Your clear blue eyes sensed every problem every trial I would see.
Your concern and guidance never varied and was always near.
You were the sun that lighted my way and made me glad to be.

With your leaving, the way forward is now darkly seen,
Dimly lit by your spark which burned so bright but which fades each day.
I can only go on with the sureness of my chosen way
Because of the love you gave freely while you were here with me.

I remember all about you
How you were always there
How it was you would forever care
How everything could be repaired but this
I remember you.

I Don't Think You Can

You say you're going to leave me behind,
Going out there to make a life of your own.
Well I don't know what you think you're going to find.
You're the least predictable person I have ever known.

I guess you are now tired of my hanging on,
That you're ready to be the one you are.
I guess you can go where you wish and when
You get there show the world that you're a star.

I don't think you can do it.
I don't think that you will.
I can only imagine you're coming back
Because I'm in love with you still.

You say you don't need me anymore.
You can do and have and be.
You can live the life you please.
No need to be as before.

You the fearless moral soldier jousting with every biased opponent,
Your unyielding brown eyes staring down each potential transgressor
Without remorse or forgiveness — no need for a Confessor.
And with metoo, the opening of doors, and the willingness to disclose,
A joy like Christmas morning thrills you right down to your toes.

Still, I don't think you can do it.
I don't think that you will.
I can only imagine you're coming back
Because I'm in love with you still.

When you roamed the backyard meditating on what God only knew
And would only smile with twin pyramid eyebrows when I asked what.
That Mona Lisa look you have that veils the mysteries within
Keeps me guessing because your dream vault is irrevocably shut.

When you went to prom in a tux instead of a gown — that was you.
When you trekked out through the desert to seek the hand carved dreams of
a lost people — certainly you too.
Your sense of the absurd always tuned to high, admiring the irony in each
sunny moment
How those before us are gone and warming their bones in the earth which
still boasts their comments.

I don't think you can do it.
I don't think that you will.
I can only imagine you're coming back
Because I'm in love with you still.

How you get up every morning to change the world to right —
How you trudged across the ridges and through the mucky swamps past the
city's blight,
Searching frantic for those failing feathered species which may have returned
And how these days you pass out so quiet in the evening as the darkness of
cabernet cools your world,
The peace of a soul worn out by good deeds, the serenity of the innocent.

I don't think you can do it.
I don't think that you will.
I can only imagine you're coming back
Because I'm in love with you still.

Now you're gone and everywhere is silence.
Not so since the day you were born,
When you came into this world your eyes were wide open
Your voice rang out clear — a resounding bell to let the world know you
were here
And nothing changed in all these years as I watched you grow until now.

I know you don't need me — I know you need to go.
I know you must needs go your own way.
Just remember that I love you.
Know that I am still here and know that

I know that you can do it
And I know that you will.
I can't imagine how I'll get along without you
But I'll always be in love with you still.

You Are What You Say

We were drifting high the night you and I brought the cheerleaders home,
No parents near and those two so excited to be with us.
I recall mostly the thrill of you taking her through the door
Leaving me with one in a tiny room learning how love works.

You and I once created reckless days that were ours to share
But now you've gone with her and I've never seen your heart so right.
You've become prismatic beyond those callow times so sweet and warm
While smoking dope and drinking Amoretto in the long dark night.

You are what you say
You are who you are
No more questions need be asked
I take you at your word for what you are and what you are going to be
No labels needed any more, only pride for all that is.

When you told me, I felt the pain in the joy, the salt in the sugar,
As you stood tall and strong amid the doubt of this imperfect place.
You've always been my best friend and now I feel the same for her.
March your own way behind the glass — shine your light for all to face.

You flamboyant butterfly, I knew you as the subtle slug with
A choice that is no choice but a destiny to be lived out.
You were the one I stayed with when I could — my friend above it all.
We hung together against the rest and never tired of hope, beauty, love.

You are what you say
You are who you are
No more questions need be asked
I take you at your word for what you are and what you are going to be
No labels needed any more, only pride for all that is.

At last you have decided to open the door and be your self
And I am to shake your hand and love you as I did before
Because nothing has changed, yet you are her and I must love you more
Since now you don't fit right upon the world's neatly straightened shelf.

You are what you say
You are who you are
No more questions need be asked
I take you at your word for what you are and what you are going to be
No labels needed any more, only pride for all that is.

We did what we needed to go and see what was and how to be.

All right then, here we go into a world I've only heard about.
Hold on tight and we'll get through each day while overcoming the doubt
Of the newby who wants to keep his head up and look the world in the eye
So when you want to walk together let's agree to never say good-bye.

He is what she says he is
No questions need to be asked
Take her word for what he's gonna be
You don't need to ask again

Rock and Ice

It's raining diamonds up there, a many faceted delight I imagine
The drops sparkle brilliant and tickle as they fall and bounce away
Tick tick tick they sound as their fall ends
Tick tick tick as they strike and they lay

Where now silent they reflect the filtered light from the moons by Saturn
And become the treasure beneath the planet's rings that orbit always
Bling bling bling from the center
Bling bling bling they shine out through the haze

Iconic and beautiful like all the billions of starry horizons
Speeding apart exponentially — fleeing one another in a counterbalanced
ballet.
Far far far into the distance
Far far far beyond today

Raining dalliant upon the drama of a human focus cast toward another world
While the warm and salty water that floats my life slows and cools
High above this world's constant bother
High above the pain endemic upon local fools

Ancient landscapes with their swirling storm fronts tracked by brilliant
inventions
Fulfilling disciplined students of atoms who gaze longingly into the
synchronized eternal afar
Wishing for fulfillment
Wishing upon each star

While I bleed down here as my old bones shrink and my weary eyes dim.
Looking out there instead of healing here — instead of supporting provincial
life, focused above

Not the best use of your effort
Not the best way to show your love

When I look up to where I am told the diamonds are falling, I cannot see the rocks nor the ice.
The face that looks back at me from the cold and the darking void expects compassion here
Life surrounds and we must shelter
Life surrounds — love those who are near.

Enceladus

In The Quiet Moment

In the quiet moment before the scream, all possibilities arise one by one.
Fear lights upon my shoulder like a translucent raptor settling in to feed.
Faith guides me toward a grimy shelter dug into the earth's dusty side.
Fate decides each movement and each moment as my eyes lose sight of all.
And I collapse into my cavernous den to await my overdue and well deserved end.
As the clock ticks on toward evening, I will soon be free again.

I am sick of death
I am sick to death
I am sick until death
In this dark place
Where no thing survives
And all that is good and all that is evil
Lives a space and then is gone
I do not know the why
And do not expect to know
So I should not care
But I wonder just the same.

Foxfire

I was there when the forest floor glowed like vigor —
Its brilliance a mystic change from dull to bright —
A chance discovery where no thing was altered but all was born in light —
Not a moon's reflected glow but a spark emanating from within —
A cool but constant effulgence that turned the mundane to delight.

I can't forget the angelic brightness within the night's dark curtained scene.
Green eyes blazing as forest floor cast shadows into the gloom,
The untouchable thing that turns the unnoticed to fascinating and unique —
A new thing not to be ignored full of a timely brief magic
That is freely given — then as quickly removed.

To have that yet again would be my greatest thrill.

But then this life ends — Its attraction disappears.
The darkness resumes as the excitement clears.
All fades along with the glow — Its fire extinguished —
Its life complete although the bodies remain.
The daylight replaces the mystic spark, overpowers the delicate incandescent blush.
Like life itself, special and delicate and brief only there for a moment then cooled and darkened, Gone as a memory with nostalgic longing — Fairies luminescence — A cool and fiery bliss no more.

I Am Alone

I am alone in a world that does not notice I am missing.
I seem to have lost my purpose here.
All that I have done is complete and forgotten.
What remains now and forward for a life that is no more?

VOLUME TWO

The Middle of the Night

I woke up in the middle of the night with cotton mouth so bad
That my tongue was stuck to the roof of my mouth.
For a moment, I thought I was paralyzed but then it pulled free.

It's always something.
I get up a bunch at night anyway.
I guess it's good I sleep alone.

There's lots of reasons for it —
The meds I have to take on an empty stomach
(Just easier to do it in the middle of the night),
When I wake up thinking about money,
The decisions I've been putting off — or you.

Sometimes my phone by the bed pings with a late night vm
So I look to make sure nobody's having a stroke or a breakdown.
It's most often a great new opportunity for a rollout awning
Or maybe a lonely Russian girl who needs help with her visa.
That calls for a drink of water!

Some nights I just can't get drowsy at all
Until after an hour or so of the therapeutic spinning of shirts at the lavendaria
Or, shocked awake, sometimes I just need to turn up the heat because my
feet are too cold.

Like I said, lots o' reasons for being awake.

McCartney says his mom came to him in a dream with "Let It Be" —
Both lyric and melody.
My mom, I guess, never looked back.
I haven't heard from her since before the funeral.

Every Moment In Life Yields

Every moment in life yields the way
Meant to steady destiny's focused sight
In guiding each step through the dizzying fray.

Lead my desultory thoughts to play
Yet a worthy role in this fight
Regardless of my tendency for delay.

When you look toward me I forget the day
And all that sets it apart from the night
Because your glance speaks more than anyone could say.

You act as the fates require and push away
Those foolish distractions, all that colored light,
Meant to cool my focus and lead me astray.

Your example allows my feeble assay
Into the next moment's subtle insight
So that I may choose the proper stay.

Don't think of me as the one who lost his way
On this pre-planned walk through the world so bright
Now that I have you to follow and to lay
Each choice down so to help me to obey.

Little Pigs

Little pig, little pig, let me come in.
You are the meal that I shall make tonight.
Open up now else I will destroy your house
Whether straw or stick or brick laid tight.

I'm knocking knocking knocking on your front door.
I hear you scurrying about like the others did before.
Your little hooded nails ticking skittish across the glassy floor.
It is the time to huff n puff
And blow the whole thing down — again.

Yes, I'm big and bad — I'm the big bad wolf,
The one your mother warned you about,
The one who was built to be hungry —
Ready to eat you up and then to spit you out.

I am the wolf.

You may turn the key to hide your selfish face
But I will be just outside trampling through the flower bed,
Inhaling all of the light and all of the air — I was bred
To work a squall upon your place.

Your chubby little self cannot escape my pursuit.
Zaftig sweet and rosebud soft you're the one that I want
To chew and savor, dripping unctuous from the spit.
Give it up — not enough bricks in the world for you to flaunt.

I'm knocking knocking knocking on your front door
I hear you scurrying about like the others did before
Your little hooded nails ticking skittish across the glassy floor

I guess it's time to huff n puff
And blow the whole thing down — again.

Yes, I'm big and bad — I'm the big bad wolf
The one your mother warned you about
The one who was built to be hungry —
Ready to eat you up and then to spit you out.

I am the wolf.

You can crouch behind or beneath — depending on how tight you've stretched
your piggy skin.
Walls can't stop me nor even dull my blast.
Start your praying, your screaming — you can plead with me or you can ask.
I'll still devour the whole of your chinny chin chin.

Build your house as big as you might
Rig up security with bright flashing lights
I'm coming with lungs filled to blow you down and away
And bring the end to your worthless string of days.

I'm knocking knocking knocking on your front door.
I hear you scurrying about like the others did before.
Your little hooded nails ticking skittish across the hard glassy floor.
I guess it's time to huff n puff
And blow the whole thing down — again.

Yes, I'm big and bad — I'm the big bad wolf
The one your mother warned you about
The one who was built to be hungry —
Ready to eat you up and then to spit you out.

I am the wolf.

It has always been this way just before the end.
You've sat to feast at the old folks' ease,
Fattened your butt, buttered your little cakes, and sweetened your tea
And after all this when I knock on your door your aim is to flee.

But you knew I was coming, as sure as the night.
You knew that nothing could stop me
So why did you turn your back to the light
And why do you call me evil when my cause is so easy to see?

I am the wolf.

Let's Fly

The world is spinning around
While I'm stuck to this unstable ground
Playing someone else's game
Where no one even knows my name
I've got to get my self unbound.

I'm feeling left out — hopeless and bored
All these people running around
While I am being ignored

Now's the time to breakout —
Like a bird in the sky,
I'm gonna fly high.
Time for me to take off
No more trade off
I won't be averse
I'll just throw it in reverse
And fly!

The years are passing me by.
Because my head is down
I never see the sky.
I'm whirling toward a breakdown
And will never know the why.

I've got to rise above.
I can do it with your love.
Come here now and let's get on out
Together.

Now's the time to breakout —
Like a bird in the sky,
I'm gonna fly high.
Time for me to take off
No more trade off
I won't be averse
I'll just throw it in reverse
And fly!

I'm going my own way.
Got my own words to say.
I've lost the will to obey
Don't care what they think's ok.
Come with me now — we won't delay.

Overcome indifference.
Move against the stasis.
Fly above it all.

Time to go — forget what's been done.
Let's just break to freedom.
Circumvent the rules.
Give all of them our back.
Speed away, be nobody's fools.

Now's the time to breakout —
Like a bird in the sky,
I'm gonna fly high.
Time to take off
No more trade off
I won't be averse
I'll just throw it in reverse
And fly!

I Will Play

I will play you my song
But it is not what you think.
For all I have are words
To tell you who I am.

Amorphous shadows float quiet
Deep down within my self.
I do not look too close
For fear that I am not what I hope.

I see but cannot describe.
I hear but fail to repeat.
I smell the scent of life
But its liquid shape evades.

Within the fading light
Sometimes I think I've found the path
And in the thought I lose my way
As sense rises to overrule.

It is the baptism of life —
The slippery baby squirms within the blessed hands
And cries of existence held back from contact,
A chance to wander through it once again.

The tree wilts in the heat of the day,
Its balance shifting hard as the axe bites again
Before it spins awkward to the ground
Never having acquired motion before.

I will play you my song
But it is not what you think
For all I have are words
To tell you what I mean...

You Are The One

The sun lights up your face while I'm still in the dark
And I'm left back when you watch the brightness complete its arc.
The rain surrounds you with a cooling mist
As I melt behind tinted glasses longing to be kissed.
You're three thousand miles away
And I think of you every day.

No no you are the one
No you're not here
But you are the one
No no you were always the one

Why must I dream of you every night?
Isn't there some one or two between here and there,
Of all the millions of loved and loving ladies,
None but you the most beautiful person I have ever seen or imagined?

A million lovely ladies — millions and more
Of all those who live nearby
So many so many just outside my door
Why is it you whom I must still adore?

No no you are the one
No you're not here
But you are the one
No no you were always the one

Take me by the hand and lead me to your self
You seeming fictive beauty of a distant life
But I can't come there.

This is where I belong.
Surprise me with your presence — continue to be my song.

When I look upon the moon's steady face
And think you're doing the same
On a cold and fearsome evening,
I imagine your look of wonder
At what I have become.

No no you are the one
No you're not here
But you are the one
No no you were always the one

I remember our time together before the lure of an eastern promise
To make your name and secure your face
The night you said your dream no longer included me
The night I was ripped from your warmth and left behind.

No no you are the one
No you're not here
But you are the one
No no you were always the one

Come and get me before I give it up
Come to love me so we can live it up
Come to join me so we won't be split up
I need you now and always — and always must.

Do you recall when we built a place for just us
And no one else was allowed — only we could trust us
But the world spun on and you rolled with it
Leaving me unbalanced, alone, and without.

No no you are the one
No you're not here

But you are the one
No no you were always the one

With you flew my purpose and like an empty pail
I'm now wobbly and likely to blow away
With the next big unexpected gust.
I need your love and your requirement
Which defines my being and is always a must.

Again

We have stepped into a Place of Fearsome Night
Again.
The Horror Of Outrage blazes across the Florid Party-Colored Script
As Black Matters Rise to speak the Sound of Reason with
The Burning Envy Of Equality in Desperate Throat Crushing Chants.

The Flash of Brilliance sparked by the Moment of the Deadly Act
Of Wrestling the Invisible Evil
Again
That knotted obstacle which represses while contemplating a solo dinner treat
Held Down by the knee on the throat, Oppressed by the knee on the throat
With Calm Gloved Demeanor while snooping accomplices sniff about the crime
But miss electric recording flung wide to all who will see.

This is the Moment Of Murder And Discovery
Again
Of Intrinsic Brutish Life beneath the Veneer of Civilized Behavior
Still closer to Grizzly than to Jesus
When we Kill Our Own Brother
Again

Because he in this Sleeveless Moment Audacious looks directly into the Eyes of Power
And is cursed for such Uppity Delusive Arrogance
Again
Because not looking down at shuffling feet
Because not pleading "Suh"
Because not submitting humble enough to please

And, with finality, because not knowing How To Endure the Breathless
Moments
While pinned beneath The Man Who Demands Death By Lynching
Again.

When the Blue Eyed Monster Hypocritic smiles quiet
Again
While piling onto the lone shackled offender
Again
Without explanation or regard
Again
Then those who see themselves as next
Must Rise Up with Daring Sacrificial Force and Speak The Need
Again

So that This Must Not Happen Ever
Again.

Cold Water

Cold water flows clean in the darkness hidden from the sun
Through time hollowed rock under the world of superficial life,
Carrying subterranean bodies blind and alien
Through the unmappable maze of beneath.

I have endured the revelation in the middle of the night.
I understand the darkness suddenly becoming light
As I see you sitting giddy at the table with your friends
Bouncing excited and pulling back as the conversation rises and falls.
What am I to do with this social situation?
How can I enter into this exclusive flirtation?

I stop your eye and become your subject for a moment.
This is as close to perfection as I have ever been.
Could I withstand the commentary of the Chosen?
Would they think I am worthy of sharing their scene?

To manage expectations, are you owned? Is that your price —
The many faceted ornament on your hand?
Are you property secured by that allotropic band?
Can you walk at will or do you go with the land?

I need to know this is more than a dream.
I need to know what you will do
If I kneel to tell you who I am
And what I would like to be for you.

I may not contradict you, correct you, or instruct you — else the magic will cease to be.

I can only follow and support you without question and with unsecured desire.

You are the one — you sailed by on a splendid sea

As I watched you circle the mist laden horizon

And enter for a moment the world that I try to understand.

Our Bernie

We voted in our Bernie
We were young and naive and vain
We elected our Bernie to the highest office in the land
We wanted a change
No more members of the arrogant and jaded elite
But a little humble smart and honest man wannabe
We elected our Bernie and then waited to see

We elected our Bernie
He seemed to be the one
Who would love us all look after the fallen and reign in the strong
We elected our Bernie
He was so gentle and kind
I hung up posters on campus and heard him admit that lust was part of his mind
Such a lack of ego so smart and honest — and blind

Then he took office and couldn't do a thing
The bad guys got worse and nothing got better
So like the southern Baptist he was he lit out for the Holy Land
To see what good he could do there
In awhile he had a peace deal in place between Egypt and their former slaves the Israelites
They shook hands and accepted their Nobels the same
While our Bernie came home with just the knowledge that he had done a good thing in Jesus' name

Meanwhile Xerxes' clan stormed our castle and took our brothers and sisters and stole our children away
They ignored our Bernie's cry for justice scoffed at our wounds and the proffered ransom

Until the new guy took our Bernie's place
Until the old guard re-entered the room
Then whether because of a secret deal or because reality demands consistency
The Old Man came in and our brothers and sisters and children came home
the same day

And we went back to canvassing and contributing more
To find another Bernie to enter again the ever swinging door
While the world kept spinning counter-clockwise just as it had before.

I Must Break Away

I must break away from reality and gather miracles to smell.
The scent of faith is lost in a crowd of those without
But you bring me a life free of the repressive rule of the many
Where your wonder wide eyes inspire and instruct me
To pass on through the open door –
To leave here without looking back —
To trade this hard place of pain and worry
For the tender loving solace that is you,
Vicariously heaven.

In me, a garbage stew confused and worthless,
You found beauty where only dirt and harsh laughter dwelt before.
My swirling ambitions ebbed and flowed
Stirred by one influence and then another.

Now the thought of you keeps me alive and
Beyond what I could have expected,
Focused upon the bright glow of your being.
You are the one who was the dream
And who now reflects the life that is we.

Wednesday is the Middle Child

Wednesday is the middle child of all of those who are.
Wednesday's child is full of woe whose wounds leave desperate scars.
From Woden comes the day's honor full, the one-eyed father of words,
And Odin the nearby cousin who shares his undaunted wisdom and crosses mutual swords
To bless the day ruled by Mercury, for those restless ones who must question all that is or imagined,
Those who must speak while discarding harsh rules
Finding their world unreliable and careless as they wander
And wonder aloud
As empathy is squeezed out by the weight of the world,
And tear wetted sadness dispersed for the others.

The Amazing Blue Eyed Cherokee

The amazing blue eyed Cherokee Indian chief at Gatlinburg
Adorned with the long and delicate crown of feathers
Where only blue eyed Indians remain
Has great prices on tomahawks and leather slippers.

VOLUME THREE

Colored Lights and Frantic Movement

I was a predestined city boy born among the sticks scattered
Back from the busy highway down a lonely dirt road to the quiet river.
The natural world held sway during those early times
Away from the colored lights and frantic movement that I dreamed of.

There the butterflies flitted fragile among the tall thin grasses
And the deep-chested birds darted between the shaded tree limbs
Of the dense dark woods that stood so very still
In their immense time and towering presence.

Because I fell into this place of slow but constant change
Where time stood quiet and seemed eternal,
My life was spent suspended within the apple branches
Above the squirming legless creatures beneath my toes.

Solemn and intense such a world lay heavily silent
While my heart beat did not match the invisible spinning.
Too much flowed within me to stay in that imaginarily static world.
It was always springtime while the sap sprinted through my veins.

Then I escaped this place sucked into the ceaseless vortex
Of streets in the caffeinated city —
A new home built of noise and constructed living
Without the song of the mourning dove — with the roaring of combusting
engines,
Colored lights and frantic movement all around.

This is where I'm supposed to be
There's no place I'd rather see
Bring me through this always swirling time
To find among all the confusion those things that should be mine.

In the city now everyone gets a turn
While the woods are ruled by the survival of the thoughtless —
Where I once lay askew among the apple branches
And jumped down on the other side
When the copperhead came to rest in the shade.

There the potent ones drink first from the pond
While the others crouch among the tall grass to wait.
There the fastest meanest strongest ones survive.
Upon the pavement those who can focus on what is not yet
Eat first and best regardless of intensity.

With no quiet here — no chance for solace or release —
Only a hectic pace while racing toward and away.
These are the days of needless frenzy
Where weakness is measured differently but still is not allowed.
Here movement is all and sitting back is the penultimate action.

I Love You

I love you
I love you
I love you
I do

I love you
I love you
I love you
For better and better

I love you
I love you
I love you
Just to be close

I love you
I love you
I love you
Forever and ever

Loving you is why I am here
Nothing else matters
Until I am worn to tatters
Until what we have becomes finally clear.

I love you
I love you
I love you
Through the thick and through the thin

I love you
I love you
I love you
To have and to hold

I love you
I love you
I love you
To love and to cherish

I love you
I love you
I love you
Until death and beyond

I've Had Girlfriends

I've had girlfriends — I've had boyfriends who I've thought were special cases.
I've taken them and been taken to many special places.
I've cried and whimpered awhile after each left me.
I've known the pain of the loss that bereft me.
But somehow I'm still standing upright
And never know the loneliness of the deep dark night.

I guess there's more for me to do.
Maybe it's finally time for me and you.
If it's not to be — if I'm not the one,
It's okay. I'm used to sleeping alone
Without love.

I've given my heart and my time along with all that I own.
Sometimes I've taken everything, opened the door, and then quietly flown.
When I see you walking toward me with those lightning eyes,
I think you could be the one that lights up my skies.
If it's so, you'll be the first
And I'll be so glad to finally be immersed
In love.

I guess there's more for me to do.
Maybe it's finally time for me and for you.
If it's not to be — if I'm not the one,
It's okay. I'm used to sleeping alone
Without love.

I'm not sure I've ever found someone to love me —
Just found crusts of bread where a meal should be
Some comfort given — some warmth as well
But no magic sparks and no ringing bells.

The world doesn't stop nor does my breathing.
Everything keeps on spinning right through the leaving.

I hope there's more for me to do.
Maybe it's finally time for me and for you.
If it's not to be — if I'm not the one,
It's okay. I'm used to sleeping alone
Without love.

The Invisible Man

You look right past me as if I am not here
You refuse to ask me what I want from you
Or tell me the things that you want me to do
Which puts you in control while I live in fear
Of what you'll think of next

A forsaken pendulum, I no longer swing
Though time continues without concern
While I watch silent hoping to learn
Though dreading that the next moment may bring
Me sucked into time's vortex

I hoped we would be the beginning of something
That might create a beautiful life
For us and to lessen the strife
While we together would long be trusting
In a world without pretext

It was the thing you said you wouldn't do
To love and to honor and to cherish me too
To see my face and to want me with you there
But now the invisible man has gone
Because you just don't care

I Have No $

I have no money in the bank nor a way to make a stack of dollars
But a tingle from the center drives my self along the road just the same.
A member of the ancient tribe of warriors I every day will get stronger —
Every day — every day for all the days there are
Until there aren't and I will go away — away — around the corner — for awhile.

Now I lose my self in you and freedom rises like the sun on the horizon.
As all things fade within the bright light of your presence,
You spur green leaves where silence was before.
You are my reason and my purpose.
You are the source of all that needs to be.
Only you matter — only you — only you.

We must agree on all that's important before that next fatal day
While the light shines and we each can still speak and be
So that life like a dream waking in the moment
May explode its self into the world that awaits.
So say what you want — what you will need
For that is why I am here. Please tell me — let me — be the one for you.

Born without mother or direction, I'm waiting for you to give and to guide me.
You are the light that brightens my world — You are the focus of my life.
For whatever lies in wait ahead, I want you next to me.
You are that which I was born for — all that I need — everything that matters.
I and you are the we that the world needs — that love needs — all that could be.

You Don't Like My Song

You don't like my song.
You look away — Well, my soul is in there.
I hold nothing back.
If you don't like it —
Then just get fucked.

So you don't like me,
Then fuck you.
Fuck you and just go away.

You think you can do better
'Cause you're smarter than me —
Younger and better looking —
So fuck you.

You've got a wife and kids and a job.
Got a bedroom for each
And those cars in the driveway —
Well fuck you.

All that ain't for me anymore. I just have words and a tune
But I can spend my nights remembering the faces in this room —
The ones who ain't you.

You can have what you got and hug them once for me
And then fuck you.
Fuck you.
Just fuck you.

I Don't Remember

I don't remember the last time we did
I don't remember the taste of your skin
Let's be together again — let's be together again
Let's get back together like we were then

I haven't seen you in such a long time
Without you baby, it's been a long hard climb

Remember when we held other every day
Never apart — a shared breath — with no rules to disobey
Nothing to say — always at play — we would just hideaway
Together

I haven't seen you in such a long time
Without you baby, it's been a long hard climb

Don't forget how much I needed you then
Let's hold hands and walk together again
Don't forget the loving good times we spent
Let's go strong and make up for the time that went

I haven't seen you in such a long time
Without you baby, it's been a long hard climb

Oh don't forget me don't forget me don't forget me no!

I haven't seen you in such a long time
Without you baby, it's been a long hard climb

We Are A Population

We are a population — a species on top of all beneath the sun
Of the genus, family, order, class, phylum, and kingdom
Who make a fire to warm us through when the world tilts away
Who morph living creations seeded or oviparous and viviparous into food
for ourselves
Who generate coverings for our bodies from creations seeded, sheared, or
processed
Who use the world's resources also for habituation and seclusive respite from
hostility
Who lonely require attention of other species, genera, families, orders, classes,
phyla, and kingdoms

Or else huddle quiet for a mate to share all that is within their reach
Radiant and strong for as long as the world remains to serve in its silent
supportive yet non-committal role
Until the illness comes and the final pain sets in — inescapable and constantly
disabling
Requiring sacrifice bold and loving without expectation of reward only relief
only the joy of having given

I'm feeding the volcano to heal the land
Here I come to end the pain
There I go to bring redemption
By feeding the volcano
Just to stop the rumbling
With hope to halt the flow
I'll feed the volcano
With my self which is what I have to give

I take the leap to save us all as I drop into the center of the world
My body, my self, going down submerged within the boil

As heated waves of dissention roil from rock strewn rivers of horror flowing down surrounding
Islands with double locks and hidden keys
All that rises is the iridescent steam of the life that's lost since nothing returns the way it entered But is renewed so that the world may not be left behind devoid and sterile.
Such a place is not our home after it all — not for long and not for ever

It is instead the assailant in profile turned askance but deadly after it all
Who will seek our destruction as we fall within its path
Bubbling and barking and running toward us in a heated froth
To tear from us our reason to make of us crippled pawns who may not stand again

I'm feeding the volcano to heal the land
Here I come to end the pain
There I go to bring redemption
By feeding the volcano
Just to stop the rumbling
With hope to halt the flow
I'll feed the volcano
With my self which is what I have to give

What If

What if you had a pain that was continuously chewing?
What if the threat of darkness was all that you ever knew?
What if movement hurt beyond your doing?
What if no one but you would ever know?
What if no end to this was determined?

You there with only the darkness —
You there with only the blame —
You there come to my side now —
You there tell me your name.

Stay To Be

The years before 30 are different than those after.
Before, you are learning to be.
After, you are trying to stay.

I've gone over the arc.
I can't do what I used to do.
Those antics are hidden behind the slope
That I speed down with geometrically increasing speed.

Joshua Tree

It's the silence at first that declares the indifference of the place
Without sirens, absent cell phones — no music or lawnmowers.
Then a sudden blur of light coats all in its orange obsession.
The panorama is immobile colored sequential by the surrounding air.

Life is there — little life — lizards, cottontails.
These skitter and hop across the surface and through the enveloping quiet
Each absorbing the character of sand and the portent of dusty scrub
Which, arid and empty of emotion, awaits the moment to strike.

With boulders scattered across its gritty girth, solid and smooth,
An old man's worried pate rises from the sandy depth
A sunning place for lizards, radiating the energy of the place
A sandy dome in a hot quiet world of suspect peace.

Here is empty and independent of thought or concern
Nearer to the stars than the moon is, closer to the end than a last breath.
Each step is laid careful — thoughtful and precise
Since the threat is real of an insubstantial, unctuous, and omnipresent maw.

One must pass through the gate with coin in hand — one final requirement
No line no waiting, no one else to ride, no others but rocks airless and hot.
We are desert sand tinted by the light of our environs
Anomalous in puddles that evaporate with each day, leaving desiccated veins
shrunken and splayed.

Sandy domes piled high become mountains of random skulls hard and dry.
These beckon the newly arrived to lounge in their minimal shade for awhile
Until the world is familiar and the light less dramatic
Until this world which is the end startles less and becomes familiar.

She Drains The Money

She drains the money out of me
Like blood from a vein
To fill a need I will never understand
As my life flows freely away.

VOLUME FOUR

Too Late Now

We looked the part of an American family
Two adults two kids a house and a four door car
A dad that worked and a mom that worked harder
Because two kids will make you older than you are

From the distance it looked like we always really cared
But nearer you could see we weren't over the rainbow
We meant to deal with it but were loving impaired
We didn't know how and there was always tomorrow

All the days we had together
All the trials we had to weather
All the rights we tried to measure
Over all the things that did not matter
Well, it's too late now

Our scars weren't outside where you could see them
But they were deep and jagged just the same
We tried to find someone out there to treat them
But there was no cure for these — only blame

We went to church every stinkin' Sunday
Sat in the quiet and prayed for better days
Living lives together but dreaming we're apart.
I finally had to leave you and take only my heart

All the days we had together
All the trials we had to weather
All the rights we tried to measure
Over all the things that did not matter
Well, it's too late now

I'm not sure today is any better
But we tried to do right on the surface
Though there was so much buried under
We could not finally come together
Because we were never the ones we meant to be

So we stand as we are — fed by the darkness beneath our feet
Facing the low sun on the horizon
As you lay waiting now under the fescue in the brown world
Beyond the blue one where we could never meet

All the days we had together
All the trials we had to weather
All the rights we tried to measure
Over all the things that did not matter
Because it's too late now

I Remember Running

I remember running toward the distant light
While those around me scatter into darkness,
Running as I must to make another flight.

Because someone's got to else we'll all go down in flames.
I'm the one to do it though you don't yet know my name.
We'll go through together 'gainst the wind and beneath the blaze
Finding our way as we struggle in the ever-mounting haze.

Running as my memories fill the air
Running as moments hurry by in flashes
Running as darkness hides whatever's there
Buried beneath the smoke and the raining ash

Yes I am still running toward the light ahead
Running to stop the danger, to quench the fear
And to rid you of all the impending dread.

I thought to myself — God Almighty, will you be there
Buried out in the distance beneath a granite prayer?
Will I see your face before the end of the long night's trudge?
Are you waiting there in cool silence to be my final judge?

Running as my memories fill the air
Running as moments hurry by in flashes
Running as darkness hides whatever's there
Buried beneath the smoke and the raining ash

Always running through this barren landscape
Of the shiny-bright frightening night,
Am I coming closer to your perfect ending?
Am I standing tall enough to pass under?

Lord, I'm running as fast as I can.
If it's not enough, please let me see
And I'll try to find a better way.

Running as my memories fill the air
Running as moments hurry by in flashes
Running as darkness hides whatever's there
Buried beneath the smoke and the raining ash

From Here I Can See

From here I can see over the golden horizon
To tomorrow's distant long waiting shore.
Little bodies scurry across the plain between here and there
Fetching and hauling, twisting and writhing — I will not miss that.
Nothing is for me but you and without you I would not be.
Thankfully you are made perfect and are set upon the world.

Turning loose and falling free of all the sharp edges
Fluttering away through still air among yellow tints
Seeing lights below as I'm nearing the end of it
Drifting slowly downward and away from you.
Whatever is there is mine forever
While you go on for now in your blue room.

What does a man do when he's no longer needed?
What does a man do when what he does is done?
Just give me a minute and I'll do what you want me to
Just another minute to do what I could never do.
You can't save my body but you can save my being,
For the words remain as long as you will care.

Turning loose and falling free of all the sharp edges
Fluttering away through still air among yellow tints
Seeing lights below as I'm nearing the end of it
Drifting slowly downward and away from you.
Whatever is there is mine forever
While you go on for now in your blue room.

Once upon a time I dreamed of being with you always.
I saw you walk away into the gathering darkness.
Your hair trailed lazily as you flipped it from your ear.

I am here for you but gravity has the final say.
I'm just an awkward old white man who knows much less than you.
If you like, you may understand me once you are older.
You may share my twilight as my sun begins to cool.

Turning loose and falling free of all the sharp edges
Fluttering away through still air among yellow tints
Seeing lights below as I'm nearing the end of it
Drifting slowly downward and away from you.
Whatever is there is mine forever
While you go on for now in your blue room.

Among The Scented Pines

Among the scented pines and the hard oak trees
In a cleared patch just big enough for rooms,
We once snuggled body warm beneath the covers
As the world outside spun on, contemplating its blooms.

That was a time of becoming before the top of the bow,
Before we let the outside pull us apart,
While home was any place we were together
Cocooning the tender focus of our joined hearts.

You were the one to come with me to be by my side
To share it all as we would deplore the world as one.
We, like each silent flower, longing to bloom forth
Lay restless while tingling with the rising of the sun.

But life is not just breath and fevered longing.
The golden sun is the air that we breathe
Until the leaden clouds quench the fiery ball
And create a blanket of darkness forcing us to leave.

Soft as the breeze, you are still the light in the darkness.
You are love without words, the reason to be.
Now I'm down on my knees with no one to hold.
Nothing remains of what was — nothing remains of we.

Today I see a flower in your hair from three thousand miles away.
I don't expect to meet you and can't imagine what I would say.
Since I don't know how to reach you, I'm going to be the person I am right here,
Unwilling to admit what I've become — unable yet to make myself disappear.

Christmas Lights

The Christmas lights are still up blinking red and green,
While they droop into darkness one by one.
It's January now but I can't summon
The strength required to go out and pull them down.
Christmas came and went — and so did you.

Christmas, with its flying reindeer expectations,
Its grinning joy and its elvish laughter —
The day finally arrives and we share it for a moment,
A brief time that fills my life with brilliant light.
Then you are gone and all the sparkle goes with you.

There's a pine forest in the corner of the room,
A dead tree with brown needles all around.
The Christmas angel stares down on me
Wondering what the hell is going on.
You walked away — now I'm just here with the tree
And the lights — I don't know how to fix this.
The cold silent darkness is killing me.

Only a dull pain in my life remains now
And timer lights that come on every night.
The neighbors may be wondering about when
But that's an answer I may not provide —
As love passes through and out of my life.

The Yuletide magic that might deliver us,
The holiday love that drew us so near,
The unexpected unforseeable of what is soon to be,
Amid the tear-filled loss of what used to be,
You were my Christmas and now you've gone away.

There's a pine forest in the corner of the room,
A dead tree with brown needles all around.
The Christmas angel stares down on me
Wondering what the hell is going on.
You walked away — now it's just me and the tree
And the lights — I don't know how to fix this.
The cold silent darkness is killing me.

I hope that what you now love, loves you back
And that your Christmases never stop coming true.
Maybe you'll remember me some day
And the joy that is gone but was once designed for us —
The wonder of all that might be on its way,
The magical thrill of being here with you.

I was dreaming that I could give you what I thought that you wanted,
Never knowing that your dream had changed your point of view.

There's a pine forest in the corner of the room,
A dead tree with brown needles all around.
The Christmas angel stares down on me
Wondering what the hell is going on.
You walked away — now it's just me and the tree
And the lights — I don't know how to fix this.
The cold silent darkness continues killing me.

In The Mud

We writhe about within the mud spiraling against black —
Kicking and screaming as the birthing pain bends us back —
Eyeless colorless thoughtless limbless creatures of the depths —
Before we crawl out and find the understanding of steps.

We've been gone so long that we no longer know who we are
Or how we came to be in this lonely place ignored yet scarred —
We the children of the children of the bastards before us
Awaiting the next line of the randomly born still without focus.

We are what we are — this is the burden of being.
We don't know why — how would you react if you knew for certain?
We are all wrong in our knowing.
A fearless love is all that matters anyway.

I have lost concern as tall buildings that block out the horizon
Surrounding my world, rise above my thought or any reason,
While the lesser I am stuck down here in the mud and the spit
That occupies my time and such small efforts as I may commit.

Never knowing how or if any of it will turn out
But certain that a storied and worthy purpose exists,
Supported by the occasional peak between the flowing drapes
That will someday open and reveal all that is or ever was.

We are what we are — this is the burden of being.
We don't know why — how would you react if you knew for certain?
We are all wrong in our knowing.
A fearless love is all that matters anyway.

Don't you recall our fecundly heartless earth mother
Who bore us from her inconstant being,
Then threatened us with her doubt provoking untouchable love
But who waits quiet to receive us when the last day comes again.

We are what we are — this is the burden of being.
We don't know why — how would you react if you knew for certain?
We are all wrong in our knowing.
A fearless love is all that matters anyway.

Staying in L.A.

I've been staying in L.A. for the last good while
Watching as the city slinks away,
Where the cars outnumber the beds today.
Blankets on upholstery, foil curtains are the rage.

I've got new scars from all this city living,
With its aching streets and its startling din.
A daylong cacophony of ringing,
Somehow I need to make this churning end.

It's hardened me and hurt me some more
To where there's mornings I don't know who I am.
On top of that no one looks at me here,
Still constantly struggling as the world spins me around.

The daylong sun has bleached all my colors out
And these shiny days have taken all I was away
While others slouch down to check the latest on their phones
And their arms carry the voices that speak the words they say.

I've decided that I'm leaving this place shortly
Going where there are people just like me
Who think the way I do while wandering together
Down a seldom used and dusty road.
When I get there, instead of sirens, I'll hear life buzzing in the fields
And maybe a bob white's call from the brush way back out of sight.

And I'll stay there with people who will care
Who might recognize me and know that I am.
Maybe if I get there I can heal some
And learn not to dread what waits yet to come for me.

I Can Do Without That

I sit cloaked here within the white walled room
With people swarming on my every side.
I see them holding hands while watching each other's faces.
I hear their voices reflected in one another's cases.
No one ever calls my name — they all just speed along never slowing
As the others come, make their claim, and leave.

The system promises to provide for them
But I'm here because I'm lost with no place else to go.
Somehow I don't fit right within their club.
I can't even force a smile through their endemic snub
And have slowed to invisible within a dimension that they may not see.
Now I don't know how or where I should be.

I'm not sure what or when this happened.
Though money never meant much to me,
I did get up and go to work every day
While my kids grew up and went away.
Now I don't have much required to do
As gray encroaches and my life begins to fade.

I guess I should have had different priorities.
Maybe I should have thought about my future needs.
But money's the thing that keeps us from what's real.
You can buy your way through life never missing a meal.
I would rather see the truth that lives in every thing.
This face is hidden and the need to see deadened by the dollar bill.

This barren last stop place will be closing soon and I will be outside.
And I'm not sure about where to go for the night.
Maybe I'll find a spot by the running water to lay.

Back in the quiet brush I should be ok.
No shoes, no shirt, no comfort required— I can get by without
Though I could use a loving one to cuddle with.

For those who haven't made it this far,
For those who are not yet tired and gray,
Then pick left, pick right — every choice affects what you will see.
Every decision made limits what you can be.
Making choices is not a choice but is required.
And, if you are able, make some friends along the way.

It's The End

We woke up in the garden in a world made just for us
It lay to the horizon and ran smooth without a fuss
Then we broke a rule 'bout eating, never thinking it was much
But when we covered up our privates there was nothing to discuss
It's the end
It's the end oh my friend
It's the end oh my friend
It's the end of the story and the time to leave is now
It's the end oh my friend

The bearded man built a boat to haul us all away
But we thought that he was looney so we told him we would stay
Then it started raining — bringing floods and winds and such
And we watched the boat sail out of sight with nothing more to say
It's the end
It's the end oh my friend
It's the end oh my friend
It's the end of the story and the time to leave is now
It's the end oh my friend

Another came to save us but we thought we were all right
He promised love and brightness to take away the night
We thought he wasn't tough enough — we want a stronger touch
Then he went upon his skyward way and left us to our fright
It's the end
It's the end oh my friend
It's the end oh my friend
It's the end of the story and the time to leave is now
It's the end oh my friend

It's the end of the story and it's time to move along
Everybody's got an itch to scratch — a choice of right or wrong
Sometimes it's hard to know exactly what to do
That's the purpose of the verses and the moral of the song.
It's the end
It's the end oh my friend
It's the end oh my friend
It's the end of the story and the time to leave is now
It's the end oh my friend

She And I

We grew up in the country way out in the sticks.
Not many people out there, only sassy rednecks and hicks
And I was proud to be one of them.

I didn't have much but I knew where I was going, sort of.
My tiny green brain refocused with each momentary shove
In a juvenile orbit of football, beer, and girls.

Down at the crystal lake, we'd meet, drink a six pack, and shoot the bull
And dive off the Southfork bridge by the No Diving sign only when the lake
was full
Where the sun kissed the water, then she kissed me, which was also against
the rule.

Lit up and rippled I wanted only to be close by,
To feel all her needs and fulfill all her just imagined wishes,
Never thinking of the future of babies and a life of dirty dishes

Because we only knew hayrides and dances,
Home by eleven or else you take your chances,
We saw only beauty in a world bent into a shape made just for us.

We were considered ignorant by older folks — sometimes to be seen but never
to be heard—
Living inside rules that others set in place, perhaps dangerous to our humanity,
Since they didn't prevent anything but just tried to corral what seemed to be
hormonal insanity.

But all that mattered to me was she brought skin with her that was like the
summer,
Soft and warm and sweet and, when we touched, things started to simmer
And I could not turn my eyes away.

When I told my dad I wanted to get married to keep her forever,
He shook his head at such a foolish idea,
Like going from dumbass kid to husband without transition,
Like building a house on the shifting sand of perdition.

A prom date turned bad, he said, looking down on me.
Might be time to say good bye to this schoolboy fantasy
And move on to college — I'd be the first from our brood —
And a career that I could imagine — coming down the road.

But this time somehow the rules did not hold
This time the force of life pushed its essence out through the leaden mold
And she and I took the vow to never change, never stray
A willing promise to face the world together for every coming day.

At the wedding, we were cute kids — me in my Sunday suit
And she all made up in her ruffled dress from the prom.
The mothers' homemade fried chicken and baked treats
Filled us with a fine ole wedding feast.
And I was off to college while she took a clerk job at the bank
Both shuffling papers all day and playing house and making love at night
It seemed ideal when we started — not much money though it all seemed
right
But soon my eyes took on new vision showing our bonds as shackles and then
my hopes just sank.

So of course dad was right — he always was and I miss him and the others
I knew then.
After the wedding and before our first anniversary I metamorphosed like a
flitting butterfly
Within a fantastic world of ancient, new, and yet to be wonders that I had
not imagined,
Having gained a new and broader outlook in a place I was walking where I'd
never been.

A university is not a place for know-it-all redneck kids who pay attention,
If they want to stay who they are — sure and settled in their certain pretension.

Such a place — home to Aristotle, Shakespeare, Sartre, et al, — was way past the narrow path
Strewn with the scattered learnings of the woods and the fields and the back seat of a car.

So I left her behind but we drowned in the flood of tears that followed this, the cruelest harm,
And in the horror that followed she made a final trip alone to the dark lake bridge and ended the fragile life I'd hurt so.
She is a memory now but her face still rises before me soft and still and warm.
I didn't understand that she would follow me every place I go.

But I remember when I touched her, at that moment my fingers came straight from my heart.
Then I could not see life without her — I could not bear the thought of us being apart.
Now these years later, I understand how life changes by the moment
But the unknowable and unteachable world stays just the same

Like memories trailing the immutable story of each life that crawls across this place,
A tale already written, lived while blindfolded and flailing within a burlap sack,
Thrown into the river, drifting away with the unseen currents of the cold dark water
Which flows into the silent infinite lake.

They say the water cleanses — it cleans away all the wrong
But I've gone down to the water and scrubbed as hard as I could every day for ever so long
And I don't feel any better about what I have done.
Tonight I'm going one more time to the bridge when the water is down
Once more to finally end my portion of this unending song.

In The Beginning

In the beginning
I went to the doctor like they say you should do.
He was poking around when I heard something new —
That don't feel right
That don't feel right
The room turned to yellow as he went down the list.
I was stunned and blinded by all of this.

In the middle
As the black hawk soars through my veins
Green sparks fly from my eyes —
The pain's a hard steel ball
That never rolls away.
It sits upon my body.
It hurts throughout the day.

In the end
They cut out my life,
Bagged me up and rolled me out,
Sent me home to live on opiods and dread
And the spinning of the scythe that hovers over me
Hisses as it turns counter to the day,
Hisses as it turns so swiftly
As I await its dropping to end all I have to say.

The drugs in my body make me dizzy and slow.
I've got to get through this somehow but how I don't know.
I've got meds to temper the slide
But the fear is mine and I cannot hide.

How will my family get by when I lay in the bed.
They would be better off if I weren't wounded but dead

So I tell no one because they'd just turn away.
With a C on my forehead I'm useless and gray,
While the A chord growls its way from the machine.
It would be better if I just went away.

Every Minute is Like Years

Every minute is like years
While waiting for something to change inside your marble head.
I don't know which hurts more — a tumor or a girl's hard glare.

Each marriage is like yours —
A challenge to survive while nodding with a quiet smile,
Giving up your life for the other who is dwelling there.

Empty minutes inspire lost years
Of opportunities overlooked or not imagined
As days rotate blindly past and you lose the strength to dare.

Emphasized modesty is limiting yourself
While others push on and forget to consider your need.
Make the noise you are here to make with all you may declare.

VOLUME FIVE

In The Name of You

In the name of you and of your boy and of all those unholy ghosts
That float through this neighborhood. Amen.
Bless me Father for I have lived.
This is not a confession since you already know all that I think, say, and do

And besides my choices are yours after all, shackled as I am by your will,
So there's really nothing to protect or plead for.

Since I have been trapped here awhile among the hoard,
I have adjudged hell to be other people,
So now I am hiding in this basement
With the door locked to keep them out.

They ignore me anyway but the noise overhead never ends,
An infestation swarming across every corner of the house.
I fear the hunger of their legs will never cease
As their squeaky voices itch my ears.

Maybe I'm a little sensitive
But I crave the quiet which now hides me in her arms
Away from these constantly moving never-evolving brutish
Two-legged insects.

When I was one of them, the noise of maddening hormones
Filled my ears with personal desires beyond any reason
Blinded as we are for most of our lives
By the scent of allure and the sight of ephemeral beauty.

It's you who are controlling the mechanism
So, if it's not too much trouble,
If it's within the rules of your game,
Please offer me solace amidst the madness
So that I may find my way back to you
In the waiting unfathomable darkness.

Where is the Electric Charge

Where is the electric charge
That runs from my brain down my spine
And triggers my heels to kick my own butt
And my soles to love the gentle touch of the tartan top?

I remember how it felt to absorb the feverish possibilities that came with the
spring.
Now I have lost the sense of this as the weather is never quite right —
Too hot or cold — too windy — too wet —
My feel for the world has devolved into a standoff
Between my own too precious expectations and what is.

And I guess that's why you aren't here anymore too.
Why would you suffer the lashes of an old man's spite
When you are so wise and wonderful
That you can see the beauty which lies beyond each raindrop?

How will I ever catch up, having paused at this indefinite life stop?

I Am Occupied By Resurrection

I am occupied by resurrection —
The older I get, the further up the cross I climb.
My head was at the footrest when I last was on the ground.

As I cling to the stubborn post, splinters pierce my uncovered hide.
Blood flows from the ragged cuts as chads of flesh dangle like fish bait.

The pain of breathing shallows by the hour and rivulets of sweat burn in my eyes.
I'm on view while the sun pours harsh light, exposing my shame —
The temporality of me displayed for all to see.

I have sacrificed my self for my others —
Those I took as mine to guide and support.
As those years flowed by, I myopic gave what I had
Until, raised up by their abandonment, I gained a different view.

Now the wonder of sacrifice surrounds me.
Choices freely made but destined to be a life
Weigh upon my shoulders stretched and feeble
As my breath fades away.

I believe there is a rest coming —
Clean white linen sheets in a cool dark place,
My scented body lying supine eternal,
Healed, spread, and minted like an Easter lamb.

I hope to be left here in peace to absorb the quiet.

We Wake Up

We wake up in the bright morning
To see all things brilliant and new.
As we sift through the world and all that's adorning
We begin to develop an individual view.

As the accumulation of moments adumbrate our new reality,
The weight of so many false turns and lost dreams
Daunt our original innocence which then twists into venality
To sluggishly flow as meandering and aimless streams.

At an unexpected moment while watching as the horizon clears,
Of a sudden motion dragging irresistible life and limb appears
And what was preface is now the story which provokes our tears
While the overwhelming and multiplying force of years
Flows hard and fast toward the end of the rapidly receding plain
And then falls splendid into the never ending darkness below.
I Know

I know you don't know me
And there's no reason you should care,
Except that I'm the one you've been expecting,
The one who can help you face what's coming
For awhile, long enough to get you there.

You are so perfect while we are so flawed.
We are all detritus while you are goddess
You, the girl in my nightly dream,
And the ecstasy measured in loving you
As I wait here to carry you up the hill.

Something as you whisper your words
Makes me listen close for the whys that are in your voice.
It makes me a little dizzy to listen as you speak.
It seems like gravity is being lifted,
As though I will never need to make another choice.

You are so perfect while we are so flawed.
We are detritus while you are goddess
You, the girl in my nightly dream,
You, an everynight magic inside lips yielding
For me to carry you up the hill

When you say my name, it is like I am born again
And nothing else matters except for me and for you.
We're a whole new thing, something I have not felt.
To touch your face again — to feel your warm sweet breath —
This is my focus — this is enough to get me through.

You are so perfect while we are so flawed.
We are detritus while you are goddess
You, the girl in my nightly dream,
I am here to marvel at your beauty
And to carry you up the hill.

I Saw Her Walking

I saw her walking ahead of me
Strolling so nicely along
With everything moving just right,
All of her motions so smooth and so strong.
Just watch as
Those legs they go to town.

So glad that I can see her.
I can't imagine missing that.
Everything inside me awakens and stirs.
Her legs go on forever and then come back again.
Everything is looking so good.
I just want to be hers.

She's taller than she oughtta be.
She sways in the cooling breeze.
I just want to stay close by
To see if she might be a tease.
Just watch as
Those legs they go to town.

So glad that I can see her.
I can't imagine missing that.
Everything inside me awakens and stirs.
Her legs go on forever and then come back again.
Everything is looking so good.
If I can just be hers.

She's shaped just like a woman is —
Endless curves and bends and what.
I'm watching 'til the sun goes down

To light up all she's got.
Just watch as
Those legs they go to town.

So glad that I can see her.
I can't imagine missing that.
Everything inside me awakens and stirs.
Her legs go on forever and then come back again.
Everything is looking so good.
If I can just be hers.

And she looks back over her shoulder
And I look right back at her.
She nods her head and we're together
And now the world is ours.
Just watch as
Her legs are going to town.

So glad that I can see her.
I can't imagine missing that.
Everything inside me awakens and stirs.
Her legs go on forever and then come back again.
Everything is looking so good.
I only want to be hers.

A Prayer

I've a question mark in my gut that wasn't there before.
I once had all the answers with nothing more to learn
Then the world crashed down around me undermining all I thought
As my life spun by afrenzy — off the course that I had sought.

You are so beautiful —
Every one of the many shapes that are you,
Perfect and feminine, capable and strong.
I would be yours and proud to be,
To walk with you toward the right and push against the wrong
If I knew how to do.

It seemed all so obvious that what is will be and remain
But now I'm sensing arcs that swirl beyond all I see.
Motion is a process that I think must never cease.

When the cold evolves into hot and the high becomes the low.
When the end is the beginning and old becomes young once more,
Then nothing that I know is certain nor is so at all.

You are so beautiful —
Every one of the many shapes that are you,
Perfect and feminine, capable and strong.
I would be yours and proud to be.
To walk with you toward the right and push against the wrong
If I knew how to do.

I thought you were here for me.
You would give love and warmth in my time to be
But all that I see spins quickly from my sight.
Nothing lasts that I find here and I cannot see a happy way out.

As all things move onward, becoming all things new,
I devolve into a feckless observer of my own life.
Though the seasons change in order and return a year away,
Life moves in uncertain directions and no one directs the day.

You are so beautiful —
Every one of the many shapes that are you,
Perfect and feminine, capable and strong.
I would be yours and dutiful
To walk with you through the right and push against the wrong.
If I knew how to do.

I'm just a wanderer who carries shadows with him on his way,
Insubstantial and cold having lost the means of loving,
Alone and confused by the light, without a constant path
And with no acceptable end in sight.

You are so beautiful —
Every one of the many shapes that are you,
Perfect and feminine, capable and strong.
I would be yours and dutiful
To walk with you through the right and push against the wrong
If I knew how to do.

Musings in the Cold of Night

With quotes from **Twelfth Night, A Lion In Winter,** & **Blade Runner**

"I was adored once," he mused as the night darkened further
And I swam in love's warm pool until the weather turned
When I began to freeze within its blustery storm,
The two of us escaped but we'd both been carelessly burned.

And like all characters of note,
He wants what he's lost though no promise can hold,
So the misery of the losing might soon be his again,
But delicate love may bring a wisp of comfort in the eternal cold.

"I am an old man in an empty place. Come be with me."
I'd take my chance again should you think love might be real
And then we could weather as one the troubling world
Together with hand in hand to serve the need to feel.

And like all characters of note
He wants what he's lost though no promise can hold
So the pain of the losing can easily be his again
But delicate love brings wisps of comfort within the eternal cold.

"All those moments will be lost in time, like tears in rain"
Once we are no longer consciously able to love.
So we should make the choice to give it all away
Because there's nothing to take from here on that final day.

And like all characters of note
He wants what he's lost though no promise can hold
So the pain of the losing can easily be his again
But delicate love brings wisps of comfort within the eternal cold.

That Old Man

I see him looking at me.
He watches as I'm moving.
I guess it's kind of creepy
But I'm hoping that he's harmless.

With a cap pulled down at his eyebrows,
A coat drawn over himself,
I wonder what he wants here.
I think he may be homeless.

That old man —
What will I do 'bout him?
That old man out there
What can I do with him?
I catch his face in the mirror.
I see his shadow crouched beside me
And in the next moment I know he is I.

I wonder what's beneath there.
Is he as worn out as his clothing?
Does he see me walking by here
Or does he just sense the motion?

He looks lost in all this hubbub.
I wouldn't notice if he weren't so close by.
He doesn't seem to focus.
He looks as if he doesn't know why.

That old man
What will I do 'bout him
That old man out there

What can I do with him?
I catch his face in the mirror.
I see his shadow crouched beside me
And in the next moment I know he is I.

I'm the one they carded way after I passed twenty.
I'm the one the girls watched walking off the field in the fading afternoon.
I can't accept this — I just don't feel it
But now I know the world has passed me by.

That old man
What will I do 'bout him
That old man out there
What can I do with him?
I catch his face in the mirror.
I see his silhouette beside me
And in the next moment I know he is I.

Live your life

The earth is heating — we can't cool it.
The ice is melting — no way to stop it.
Mad men rise and just as quickly fall
As outraged observers barbarically howl.
Don't make yourself crazy following this all.
No one knows long term what it will bring.

Live your life — love the loving.
Let everything be what it's destined to be.
Make your day scream with delight.
You have still until the night
And then it all just spins away.

Those things that are born must surely die.
That's just the way it's set up to work.
You win some when fate says you can —
You lose some when you're supposed to fail.
It all has to balance at the end of your day
So go on out, find your spot, and play!

Live your life — love the loving.
Let everything be what it's destined to be.
Make your day scream with delight.
You have still until the night
And then it all just spins away.

The world turns round without your pushing.
It will do so long after you're gone.
Remember that love is the answer to the question.
Follow your heart and sing your own true song.
It doesn't matter how hard you may cry.

Make the most of what you are given
And take the path that lights your way toward heaven.

Live your life — love the loving.
Let everything be what it's destined to be.
Make your day scream with delight.
You have still until the night
And then it all just spins away.

Hold My Hand

Hold my hand because I love you.
Hold my hand — come and go with me.
Yes there's lots of stuff out there.
Yes people will try to hurt us.
If we take our steps together,
None of it matters
Because we'll just walk on through it all.

We'll go side by side
So nothing else will matter.
Whatever happens, we'll face it as one — with a smile like a W
Making the difference between life and living
As the steady heat of our days passes on by.
We'll stroll through the meanness, the tragedies, the ultimate loss
Holding our hands through it all.

Hold my hand,
Our fingers entwined as are our lives.
Hold me tight like our future depends on it.
Nothing else will matter.
Whatever happens we'll face it together — with mutual delight.

Hold on like you mean it.
Hold tight through the wind and rain.
Hold me — keep us together.
Don't look away — we'll go on in spite of the pushback
And love the feeling of each arriving moment.

On That Day

On that day, just drag me out by the ankles
And leave me by the street with the stripped down Christmas trees
And the soiled ratty sofas with exploded cushions like shotgun wounds.

VOLUME SIX

I Can't Be You

I know you're right
Your choice is the thing you should do
But your life is your own
And I can't be like you

You can point your finger
And wag your tongue 'bout me too
But I'm going down a different road
'Cause I can't be like you

Oh no, I can't be you
I can't can't can't can't can't be you
Oh no, I can't can't can't can't can't be you
I can't can't can't can't can't be you
No, I can't can't can't can't can't be you

It makes no sense to compare your life
to another
Your task is yours — your pleasure your own
The rest of us are following our pathways
Which are all divergent as we each find our way home

I get up in the morning and see the world my way
The enslaught of color and sound
Attack me all the day as time comes slowly into focus
And then I can begin to find my way around.

Oh no, I can't be you
I can't can't can't can't can't be you
Oh no, I can't can't can't can't can't be you

I can't can't can't can't can't be you
No, I can't can't can't can't can't be you

Words are hurled in my direction
Some kind — others meant to sting
My job is to work my way through them
And to find what good my life may bring

Oh no, I can't be you
I can't can't can't can't can't be you
Oh no, I can't can't can't can't can't be you
I can't can't can't can't can't be you
No, I can't can't can't can't can't be you

I'm Headed Back

I'm headed back to Carolina where the lights are going out one by one
For years I've been as far away as I could be but the growing darkness draws
me back again
I'm all alone here — and there I guess I'll be the same but I'll be home

You can't go home again they say
I don't look like I did but I feel like I do
Maybe the place I left is like that too
Perhaps it will be ok

Their sun I think still drifts lazy across the sky over a place beautiful and still
And the stars at night swing above the crickets and the lightning bugs as the
cemeteries fill
I left early on a mid-summer day after you had packed your bags in a huff
and gone away
Not knowing where you would be I just drove on west until the road ran out
and stayed
That was a long long time ago

You can't go home again they say
I don't look like I did but I feel like I do
Maybe the place I left is like that too
Perhaps it will be ok

I remember flying low over the woods and fields where nobody can be seen
Above the blinking ribbon of the river flowing out of sight
I am so lonely now with no one near in this cold silent place
I hope that you might be there somewhere to hold me and to add to my life
a smiling face
I wonder if you're there at all if you have a family how you may remember
loving me

111

You can't go home again they say
I don't look like I did but I feel like I do
Maybe the place I left is like that too
Perhaps it will be ok

He Was The One

He was the one I focused my hate upon
Because he took my love from me.
Of course, she was not the one to blame.
I know she loves me still today.

Tall and mean, he would not look away
And she fell into the darkness of his eyes.
I told her I would kill him if I ever saw him again.
She looked blankly back as if she did not understand.

How could I go on loving while looking over my shoulder?
Wouldn't the evil just keep growing bolder?
I could not stand the constant presence of his lurking form.
I was raised to bring on the light, not to turn my back,
Nor to run from the life defining fight.

I saw him at the club doing shots with his usual sleazy crowd.
His sneer spread across the room like the dread that he was.
He had no sorrow nor was he afraid he told me with his serpentine hiss
So I cut him between his ears with my knife
And then I watched as the evil one bled.

Maybe she and I could have worked it out between us
But I thought his insolence was nothing we could forget.
I felt the need to cleanse our magical world of the threat
Of the looming depravity of him.

How could I go on loving while looking over my shoulder?
Wouldn't the evil just keep growing bolder?
I could not stand the constant presence of his lurking form.
I was raised to bring on the light, not to turn my back,
Nor to run from the life defining fight.

But now I am alone in this cold hopeless place
And soon I'll walk just one time more.
As now I hear other voices echo against the walls,
And wish I could fly from this cage to her.

I've had a birthday all my life and now there's a deathday too —
Another number to place upon the stone
Above the scarred earth soon to be my home
Beneath the baffling place that I have wandered through.

How could I go on loving while looking over my shoulder?
Wouldn't the evil just keep growing bolder?
I could not stand the constant presence of his lurking form.
I was raised to bring on the light, not to turn my back,
Nor to run from the life defining fight.

I live for her, I breathe for her —
The warmth of her touch feeds my soul
And gravity gives way to light
As we merge to a single whole.

Funny I haven't heard from her.
I'm unsure of where she'll go from here.
Now together with my little two legged dreams I am locked up
In a room with no way out.

How could I go on loving while looking over my shoulder?
Wouldn't the evil just keep growing bolder?
I could not stand the constant presence of his lurking form.
I was raised to bring on the light, not to turn my back,
Nor to run from the life defining fight,

Why would there be a law against ridding the world of bad?
Aren't we supposed to stand up and protect those we love?
I only did what was necessary to make my home a better place
And, now that it is, I am not allowed to stay and enjoy the peace.

Out My Front Door

Out my front door is a walkway where — all throughout the day — people stroll hand in hand or jog alone.
It's kind of annoying — the constant motion and the passing voices that erupt as they go along.

Then there are steps that drop to a concrete bike path — equally busy
With cyclists and scooters both to and fro — sometimes laughing, others intent — on either side of a red striped line.

Then past that lies the sand — uncountable grains, warm and clinging — inviting quiet repose
And then finally I guess there's the water — constantly becoming and retreating — cool and opaque in its patient and timeless dance.

I've never known what lies beyond the water —
I'd tell you if I could.
If you decide to leave, I'll google it and then can give the answer — to myself.
If you decide to stay, I'd rather spend my time looking — at you
And continue to live — never knowing what's beyond the dancing water
And that will be all right — with me.

When I Was There

I am just an awkward old white man
Who's lived every day where I am.
I am not a politician.
I don't care what anyone thinks of me.
I am what God made me to be.
I follow the path She has laid out without question.
My early days went like this —

I was just arrived when my mother gave me up to the Baptist Children's Home because she was a high school student and a poor orphan who had her own life to figure out. She never told my father that I was.

I was part of a new family when Christmas mornings came and presents filled the living room where the decorated tree was. It was wonderful. The four of us spent every Sunday morning at the Methodist church that my mom had grown up attending. We never missed a service.

I was there when Bob the old black laborer sat on my parents' back porch eating his fried chicken lunch on a paper plate with a fork my mom would throw away when he was finished. Then I went inside and watched on the black and white TV the first astronaut launched blindly into space and wanted like every other little boy to follow that path too some day.

I was at school the Friday that President Kennedy was killed. Mrs. Pressley the librarian came into the classroom to tell us as much as she knew and we prepared to duck and cover as our teacher bowed her head and wept. But when his killer was killed himself on Sunday we didn't know what to do.

I was there when Gary, the black kid whose dad kept the doctor's office in Claremont running, showed up at my high school one day and said he was now a student there. Ok, do you play football? Gonna eat that apple? Later I

116

saw in the newspaper about the two hundred U.S. Marines who were reported killed yesterday in a place in Asia that none of us had ever heard of before.

I was there when my cousin Randy reached down into the dark hole of the split cedar tree and pulled out an owl that looked at us for a moment and then flew away. Since there was no owl season, we let him go. Then we shouldered our shotguns and walked on through the woods with our pockets full of dead varmints.

That was the same cold bright winter day that he walked across the frozen creek and looked back at me to follow. I knew as if I were already wet that I could not do so but tried and of course sank up to my knees in creek water with my first step and slowly froze until we completed the hike back to Uncle Vince's fireplace.

I was there when the black kids no longer walked through the other door that led to the balcony at the State Theater on Saturday afternoon but now walked in with the rest of us and we sat and ate popcorn together and laughed at the silly antics on the screen. None of those kids showed up for school the day Martin Luther King, Jr. was buried — we were jealous.

My number was 177 but I was a 4F college student until I dropped the deferment for a 1A out of guilt that those of my buddies both black and white with single and double digit numbers were already gone. When Ray's brother came back in a box amid rumors of friendly fire, we started to question the cost of the endeavor.

I sat in a room when the L-R honors English professor wrote for us on the board — Beginning to learn is beginning to be undermined. Now write for an hour or until you are finished. That was the first college test anyone in my family had ever taken.

I didn't have a motorcycle but Randy had an old Triumph with faulty electrics that shook the ground when it came near. I was going to bed the full moon night of August 25 when the sirens and red flashing lights came up the road toward the hospital with Randy in it. Either the lights went out or he turned them off under the guidance of the full moon. His dad sold the bike for scrap.

My college classmates and I pushed for our chosen savior to go to Washington to straighten out the crooks and to clear a better path for us all. We even got him elected. But when he could not navigate the sacred halls of enducement he retreated as any southern Baptist would to the Holy Land to negotiate a peace — and then watched as the guys he soothed into agreement walked away with the prize while the Middle East Great Satan took our children and held them until the end just as our own Great Satan was inaugurated and then proceeded to make ketchup a vegetable in school lunches.

Then mom got Alzheimer's and soon didn't know my name, then later couldn't tell me what she knew, then finally curled up and died in silence. A little dead bird, hers was an awful journey.

I left the morning of July 24 with what I had — my weight bench, some t-shirts, a shoebox with $6,000 in twenties, and a six pack of Dixie that I'd been stopping a door with. I left my dreams there as I turned my back on everyone I knew or had ever known. It was the right thing to do.

I remember these things and have forgotten many more from those early years that have shaped how I see life even now.

Size Twos

His size twos were still warm inside when I picked them up from the pavement
Still tied in the double knots that his mom sent him out in
Not a scratch on them where they lay on the crosswalk
While his little self did a perfect flip through the air soaring all the way to heaven

He was moving always moving
He would run around the room so fast that even Sparky was confused
Now he is endlessly still terminally quiet
His eyes half open through his black-framed lashes as if in a brown study
Never to open wide again with the joy of a new red bike

The compact driver paused a heartbeat before darting from our sight
I guess he doesn't care about lives outside of his car
Maybe there are others that bring happiness to him
But in the receding taillight glow, we have only a limp little boy to remember him by

Who was moving always moving
He would run around the room so fast that even Sparky could not keep up
Now he is endlessly still terminally quiet
His eyes half open through his black-framed lashes as if only in a daze
Never to open wide again with the joy of a new red bike

With his shaggy COVID haircut and the smoky quartz of his eyes
He was the life of our building the joy of our block
I don't know how we can do without him
Our world is now robbed of dreams and delight
They were stolen by a careless thief just last night

It's a moveable world where motion may describe a lifetime
Where responsibility exits when the cost seems too dear
We've forgotten the promises made for our freedom
Leaving it to us to bear the guilt or hold the sorrow

He was moving always moving
He would run around the room so fast that even Sparky could not keep up
Now he is endlessly still terminally quiet
His eyes half open through his black-framed lashes as if only in a daze
Never to open wide again with the joy of a new red bike

I want to pull the covers over him and to kiss him goodnight
But he's not tucked into his little bed and the sky is flashing red and blue
While the sirens scream at the horror lying here below
To kiss him goodnight and to a final time turn out his light

Murderous steel arrived unexpected
To a life surrounded by stuffed animals and toys
A thoughtless intruder scurrying by
An unseen threat to unaware little boys

I look for the little guy behind every doorway
His smile once lit every corner of every room he scampered into
I'm afraid the sun will no longer shine for me
There is nothing I can do about the curse of metal the fragility of life

Consequence of action
Run from the mistake
Whatever else comes it's the end of the day
Both distracted and impaired
And now it seems that concern for others is insincere

When We First Met

When we first met, I thought you were the most stylish girl in town.
You had frills and labels — all you needed was a crown.
I don't know why you noticed me among the jeans and t-shirt set
But I was happy when you did — you're the chichiest girl I've ever met.

But time has its way of eroding life's little differences,
Enlarging them as we go into chasms of uncrossable distances.
So I guess we've come to see such affectations divide us
Until both of us would like to see someone else beside us.

Gucci Prada Chanel Dior
Inamorata Burberry Hermes Fendi St Laurent
It's an elite and different language from another land.
I don't think I can learn it. I just don't think I can.

You don't like my sweatshirt or the way I comb my hair.
My shoes are not shiny and my pants are baggy in the rear.
You don't want to be critical but your face is turning red
And I'm thinking about placing this wine bottle somewhere near your head.

I don't guess there's much love left here for us to show
So maybe I'd better take my wrinkled self and go.
You're perfect in your fashion sense and where you decide to show your face,
While I wear my favorite jeans and a T to the theatre and to any other place.

Gucci Prada Chanel Dior
Inamorata Burberry Hermes Fendi St Laurent
It's an elite and different language from another land.
I don't think I can learn it. I just don't think I can.

I've heard all my life of opposites attracting,
Like the divergent poles of a magnet that are reacting,

121

But I don't see how that could ever be true
Unless steel is easier to get along with than are you.

Gucci Prada Chanel Dior
Inamorata Burberry Hermes Fendi St Laurent
It's an elite and different language from another land.
I don't think I can learn it. I just don't think I can.

The World is a Beautiful Place

The world is a beautiful place.
I've seen some of it — most of it not!
Its wandering rivers, its green shady valleys, its deserts and plains —
Sometimes I am stunned by its beauty.

I feel a part of it — like it is my mother who is made of the same stuff as I.
Living with its cycles and within its self — I am both its child and its spouse.

Soon I will not be here which is the part I do not understand
But I know I will still be — freed of my form and senses and the pressures
of living
And with only the truth, whatever that is, remaining and remaking the one
that was I
Into something universal within the real world that is my own.

Sometimes I feel a tingle that begins in my toes and turns red my fingers and
my ears —
A thrill to be alive — what a wonderful place to be.
Sometimes I forget the hard rains and the bitter cold days that I've endured
beneath shelter —
For when the spring comes all is right and nothing bad remains.

I think that I will miss it — then I remember what is ahead and know this
is not true.
Through the inevitable inescapable doorway lies an eternal light and beauty
that will not be denied.
This is but the shadow of what awaits without fear or anger, dread or desire.
I know that such a place outside of time and raindrops will be mine in awhile.

Let's Do It Again!

Let's do it again!
Let's pretend the day's beginning and everything is green and new.
Let's hold each other tightly and dare the world to bully its way through.
I can't slow down 'cause then the thinking sets in.
If I ever stop doing, I don't know if I can get going again.

Let's do it some more!
I haven't lost the need or the wanting.
The sun's not gone down yet
And your lips are awaiting.
You're all that's mattered to me ever since we met.
Let's go on together and see where we can get.

Will you wash your hair tonight?
Are you staying in as well?
Will you put yourself to bed alone?
Will there be anything to or not to tell?

Instead, let me hold you quiet away from the crowd.
Take me with you to the world that you have made.
I want to be the only one you look for in the night.
Let me hold you and I promise to be there by your side.

I just need you to love me.
I hope you'll always be here.
I don't know what you want next
But I think I'm lost until you give me your kiss.

I'm not sure what really matters — it's never been clear to me.
I feel like love is the answer — it is up to us to see.
Yours is the life that I have dreamed of,
One without the failure that is mine,
You above the lies — you so capable of love.

It All Begins And Ends With M

It all begins and ends with M.

Maybe more means warm esteem minus decorum.
Manic mayhem maximizes hoodlum tantrums, minimizes pacifism.
Charm mainstreams magnetic magic.
Ransom may redeem mean system.
Arm vandalism — master grim alarm.
Poem inform racism.
May kingdom socialism confirm team asylum.
Man reform, maim messy intellectualism.
Helm pacifism, scream revivalism.
Martyrs affirm delirium.

Daydream upstream — decorum proclaim doom.
Odium glooms denim romanticism.
Messy merits my custom wisdom.
Mod mini mode makes ballroom reform.
Many mobs swarm, master hoodlum boredom.
More matters, men mark.
Millenium means male, many moan.
Minimum maximum — freedom pacifism — optimism sarcasm
Farm grim esteem.
Redeem movie elitism.

Love neither begins nor ends with an M
But it does.

You Told Me You Were Leaving

You told me you were leaving
On a call at dusk on a lonely Wednesday in March
While the wind was hard blowing
And the little life exposed cried for shelter from the bitter storm.

Then spring came but it made no difference
No warm rains, no flowers startled into bloom
Only the spinning — the never ending dizzying spinning —
Gathered darkly to further spread my gloom.

After you left, each sunset became the beginning of another end.
Every day I remembered what was no longer here
And the worst of it is still the weekend —
On empty Sundays it's dark a long time before the sun goes down.

I counted on you to give me a reason to be here.
I found in you a warmth to help me through my day.
I loved the things you loved, gave up the sharp corners,
And became what it seemed you wanted me to be.

I see your face in the midst of every group of people.
I think you must be there — you always were.
I hear your voice in a crowded room, but it's not you there.
You're gone from here.

Love is not supposed to fail — I gave you all I had, all I was.
What did I miss? What was just not enough?
What more — what else is there more than this has been?
I'll try to shore up these walls that hold me in my place

And await someone else to reform my mind.

I Never Liked

I never liked the curving boards,
The filigree, the moulded curls of pine.
It seemed the mistress's house
The master left behind.

VOLUME SEVEN

You Don't Seem To Be Happy

You don't seem to be happy
With your face turned toward the wall.
Is it something I said or should say?
Would you like to dance and forget about it all?

I can try to be better.
I'm just learning what you are like —
What turns you on, what turns you off.
Lady, rising to your summit is turning into a hike.

Nothing that a little touch wouldn't fix —
Beyond thought, a dream's tingling rush —
The thought of you lying next to me!
I've such a terrible crush!

When we met at the bar with your friends swarming around,
I couldn't get a word in until they drifted away.
Then I asked you to dance and we were alone within the sound,
Facing each other, our bodies came together as it played.

What can I do to keep you happy?
Would I make a silly face like a clown?
Should I stare with meaning, raise one eyebrow or maybe pull it down?
Might I merge my expression with yours and follow your every glance?
Well, here we go, maybe I can — let's see how long we can dance.

But remember that when life becomes music,
If the song loses its beat,
Then what's left is drifting through uncharted places,
Where we'll need to step carefully together to discover our own faces.

When She Said Good-Bye

When she said good-bye,
It was a near fatal blow.
Who said words can't hurt?
What a callow foolish statement!
I am crushed — hope gone, nothing more to know.

We fell — she took me down hard and turned,
Broke my bones and shook me up some.
I guess she just didn't want to be here anymore.

When the dust settles,
Maybe I can love you,
When I can see again,
See my way again
Back to the one I thought I was,
To the one I want to be once more.
Maybe I can love you then
But not right now.

I know you are not she,
That you see me as the one
To make your life complete,
To be the one you want to come home to,
A partner who will love and touch and be.

But my strength is gone.
I need some time.
Healing is the task before me
Since she took all my breath away.
She was my past, has abandoned my future,
And steals my now.

When the dust settles,
Maybe I can love you,
When I can see again,
See my way again
Back to the one I thought I was,
To the one I want to be once more.
Maybe I can love you then
But not right now.

She slowed time so much I could feel my breaths between the ticking of the
clock.
I could feel my blood oozing through my veins —
Slowly, sluggish, lifeless, and cold.
This is the end of everything I have loved.

When the dust settles,
Maybe I can love you,
When I can see again,
See my way again
Back to the one I thought I was,
To the one I want to be once more.
Maybe I can love you then
But not now.

I Guess It's Time To Go

I guess it's time to go on around.
I'm not sure when or why but soon.
Don't yet know how but time is slowing down
As am I so the end must be just over there.

I feel like I woke up on Saturn
Where my body is beneath the sea.
My feet are stuck to the floor.
Moving used to be easy
But it isn't anymore.
I hate gravity and what it's doing to me.

I live on an electron spinning through infinite space
Reflecting the light of the universe with my tiny warmed up bulk.
The proton that holds us near is hot and bright and strong
And provides us the light and the way to spin out our brief scurrying ways.

All the laughing and the crying,
All the winning and the losing, all the right, all the wrong,
Who will care of it, who will know of it
In the coming lifetimes when we are gone?

I see the wavy colors of the forest.
I feel the heat of the summer day.
I smell the scent of you beside.
I taste the cool golden wine that sits before us.
I hear the wind moving the branches of the backyard poplar trees.
Who will remember all this when we are cold and still — will our selves then
be free?

I guess I can do without knowing this
And imagine I'll find out then.

Now I live for the summer like the red apple tree
Reaching toward the sun, my arms filled with a fruit offering.
July is my moment — that's my time to shine
Brightly all day and into the night.

I Met You In A Crowded Room

I met you in a crowded room,
Beer bottles clinking and an annoying buzz of voices.
You walked right up and started talking.
I was startled because you had so many other choices.

I was just one in a line of meat and beer,
One you could choose or pass on by,
Something like being on display
Among my equally numb and needy peers.

It was a phase I had to go through,
Nothing I want to dwell on now though
Because it's time to go on
Since you've started to grow with me.

She had moved on what seemed a lifetime ago.
I thought we were together as one forever
But something I did or should have done pushed her away.
She left the details spinning in the air.

How can a light that shines so brightly — so warmly and so rightly,
How can such a joy die so quickly and the life retained
Become so worthless and unlikely to regain?
Why would I wish to crawl through this and remain?

It was a phase I had to go through,
Nothing I want to dwell on now though
Because it's time to go on
Since you've started to grow with me.

Just another phase after all though it seems so real
I'd have thought I would never reattain the feeling —
The tingle of your warm breath and the allure of your smile.
Just to be near you may be the start of healing.

As the jonquil blooms in the springtime
After a cold and hurtful season,
So it dies again in the autumn
And awaits the warmth to rise again toward completion.

It was a phase I had to go through,
Nothing I want to dwell on now though
Because it's time to go on
Since you've started to grow with me.

The Great Depression

We ate cornbread crumbled in our milk, mayonnaise on cherry jello for dessert.
Sometimes mom added well water to the soup to make another meal.
We found that any portion of a pig will fry — nothing goes to waste.
We went out hunting rabbits and mom baked squirrel pies in season —
Tastes like chicken but sometimes a little stringy.

We would dig at the creek banks for turtles, wading up to our waists
And would fish for hours at a time in the late afternoon, taking bass and crappie from the Catawba.
We planted corn, green beans and tomatoes — loved to eat fried chicken, bacon, and roast beef.
We could grow it and can it, raise it and slaughter it for the kitchen table
Living off the land and the riches that it could bring.

My brothers and I spent our nights together under Grandma's pile of quilts
watching the stars shine through the roof of the old home place
And were up and dressed real quick when the east began to light.

Our treats were apples and pears in the summer, warm right off of the tree.
We'd have chicken and dumplings for Sunday dinner,
Same again for supper until it was gone.
There was always a pitcher of tea in the ice box
And often biscuits smelling warm in the kitchen.

Feeding chickens, gathering eggs, milking cows, and murdering hogs
Always gave us something to do
And maybe some school to go to too but not in the summers.
That was spent plowing behind a mule (Bob the first and then the second) in the muggy blue toned blaze,
Planting and gathering for the winter like the squirrels that weren't yet shot.

Dollars were scarce but good times were still there.
We'd gather around the wood stove or on the porch depending on the weather
And play a country song or two, feeling it out with our guitars, banjos, and fiddles.
Mom would play the piano too.

Sometimes I'd ride Bob to town on Saturday after plowing him all week
And we'd all walk to church on Sunday with our ties and with shined up shoes on our feet.

Talk about your food insecurities but we never knew the term.
It was just a part of our lives with all of our world to affirm.
Such demands were constant but fair.

Living among the black folk who were as hamstrung as we,
Playing and laughing together at a time when none of us were free
But chained to the land with our brothers for as far as we could see.

We never noticed the difference until we went to town together
Where the Beatties had to go through the side door at the State Theater.
They'd watch the movie from the balcony while we sat below.
It seemed oddly familiar but how were we to know —
Just country bumpkins — we not ones who made rules but who trudged forward left right left right
And after we'd get candy at the Woolworth's where they only had one door.

Ole Tige would be hungry too if I was, his rabbit chasing days gone by,
But he was still a fine companion when you tossed him some left overs and could get him to moving again.

As I look back over these lines, I see that they are mostly about food
The securing of which was our primary occupation
But there was love too — I know there was — love and kindness that was always just assumed.

Hey Kids!

Hey kids! We didn't used to do it that way.
We found that kisses could bring tears instead of joy.
Though asking wasn't cool,
It was a better way to enjoy.

Hey kids! We did it this way
Because a lover can be a friend as well.
We found it wasn't easy not to tell
But things went smoother without ringing that bell.

Hey kids! We were influenced by courtly love —
Holding up the beloved
So she could shine brightly in the sun.
Love is not a race nor is it a game.

Love is a dedication made without a price —
A ceremony with a bowed head
And respect for another life
Who may be willing to share time and self with you.

Of course there were also those whose desires were uncontrolled,
Who would focus only on the taking with no regard or respect.
These were not admired — but left behind as the world spun on,
Not idolized nor followed but forgotten after the tingling stopped.

Well, kids, maybe we did it just like you.
Only the clothes have changed —
Just the language of the street
And the cars that take us there.
Maybe it's all the same —
You and I and the world we travel through.

When I Look At Your Eyes

When I look at your eyes, I forget where I'm going and what I'm supposed
to do.
When I see you walk by, your synchronized motions make me believe
There's nothing more graceful in the world than you.

You are the answer to every question, the origin of all that's good.
I could never have imagined your beauty — no I'm sure I never could.
Being with you is the most fun I've ever had standing up
Or lying down.

Please don't ever go away — that would surely put me beneath the ground.

We Stand Alone

We stand alone focused upon our selves until love appears.
The only force that can lift us out of the dark purpose,
Love makes it easy to care about another.
Love rights the listing ship, saves the lonesome unworthy,
And brings the world together and along.

I saw your face but could not speak —
Your life was so much different than mine.
I've been working ever since hard to make my way
Into the room where you might take a look at me.
Sometimes it's seemed much more than I can do

Yet I feel a subtle progress as I climb through day by day.
I sense the morphing of my own self into one that may be worthy
As I work my way toward you and your consequential light —
"But there are a lot of broken hearts in here —
4 or 5 years is a long long time."

There can be no dissembling — there can only be the trembling
That brings me to life — into your life —
Into a life that matters more than I ever would alone.

Why is it?

Why is it you are laying there?
It's time to be up and moving
While all else is flying through the air.
Careful or soon you'll be left behind.

The race for what is there to harness
Begins and moves from within.
You must grind to succeed regardless
As a casual approach will never win.

Of course succeeding, they say, is all or else.
You can't just stand and observe.
Chasing butterflies and smelling roses
Will not get you the reward that you deserve.

Concrete and splinters are where forests used to be,
Smashed and scattered by the vanity stampede.
We know how to do so much.
We do not ask if we should.

Parents and teachers put up the bumpers —
No way for a kid to lose the race.
All is allowed from the time they're in jumpers.
The results of their acts will some day smack them in their focused faces.

Why isn't there?

Why isn't there a road map,
Some signs along the way? —
Stay away from this one
Or cuddle close and hope she'll stay.

Maybe it's my eyesight —
I don't seem to get the drift
Of good and bad that's floating by.
The world just turns so swift.

I've always felt like red meat tossed into the lion's den
A lean shiny steak just lying inert.
Exposed and silent, I'm ready to become the next meal,
Without a sense of direction, destined to be meticulously hurt

I know you're out there someplace.
You may be as confused as I am.
Maybe you're looking for me too
For us to become a wonderous poem, not just a passing epigram.

I see you in the night time.
You're to be the story of my life.
You represent the hope that you and I are.
Your love is to be the end of strife.

You Saw The Armies

You saw the armies coming.
You saw the homes ablaze.
You saw the long guns wielded.
You did nothing. You did nothing at all.

I remember everything.
I can forget none of it.
I should not have been there.
I did nothing. I did nothing at all.

Because you could not bring yourself,
Because I thought myself too young,
The sun went down, the moon came up
And we were lost again.

While you lay down curled up and unconscious
I drove until the road ran out
Way beyond the river
Well above the mean.

Waiting for resolution is not
Working toward a right solution.
Your life should be worth
The effort to reign in the conflict —

As the guns fire from the church spire,
So that God may live forever.

Clown or bully is our choice —
Singing for love
Loving the song
Living and singing along.

Giving the wall or marching stiff legged on
We must choose an ideal to seek
While that which combines us
Pushes each further away.

I Don't Want To Be

I don't want to be the teacher.
I don't think I know enough to intend.
I've given up concerning the why
That stands between here and my end.

VOLUME EIGHT

It is Now Midsummer

It is now midsummer and your beauty is ripe
Your hair thick and sweet like the hay being gathered from the fields
Your face and hands as soft as apple blossoms
Your mind as bright as the eternal sky above
Nothing exists that can outshine you
You are quick and alive a special gift unto the world
Yours is the perspective of perfection
Your beauty derived from the warmth of the summer sun

But the world continues turning
And the fall is on the way
Summer blossoms will fulfill and then must transform and die
What to do while you are blushing
How to spend these precious moments
While the warm sun shines before life and beauty fade away

Do You Feel My Hand

Do you feel my hand on your arm?
Do you sense the warmth I offer?
Can you feel my hand on your arm?
Can you forget the world surrounding us?
This is my hand upon your arm.
I feel you tremble now.
An irregular shuddering now rises
And narrow slits have replaced your eyes.

Why are you trembling now?
Do you think you might stay?
Do you think the morning will be just another day
Or will tomorrow bring a new found light
To shine down on both of us as one
Who will live then forever beneath a new and loving sun?

We Met By The Steps

We met by the steps that led down to the grassy lawn
Surrounded by oaks under the new spring sky.
I remember feeling the lift of that beautiful day,
A sense of flight as gravity's force just drifted away.
Her eyes sparkled in this different pale light.
I asked her to come with me
To see what the world might hold in store.
She took my hand and we began to soar.

Why aren't you out there doing
What you know you ought to do? — she said,
As the sun arced over the empty blue sky.
Suddenly the light shone through my cloudy brain
And I realized the road in front of me
Which I had only rarely sniffed before.

Grandpa Bennie Was The Baby

Grandpa Bennie was the baby of the brood.
Things were tough back in the Depression.
Nothing was surplus, not warmth nor sleep nor food,
Except for the multiplying mouths of the brood.
Grandpa Bennie with Miss Veda on the piano
Would pick the 6-string and everybody sang
The best they could while Lucas would saw across his fiddle
And Robert would beat that ten gallon tub.

When the radio came, music tagged along with it
And they all got to hear sounds they'd not imagined before.
It was life-changing, an entirely welcome visit
And brought them into the world through a previously unopened door.
It was just the beginning of course —
The new was an unstoppable force.

A Bottle of Love

First comes the tingle as the cold liquid flows and spreads
That wakes up the spirit and lightens our suddenly fearless heads.
Then arrives the warmth that overwhelms outside circumstance
And raises up the blood into an urgent need to dance.
Next enters the numbing of extremes and the overall wobbling
Which precedes the loss of external focus and precipitous squabbling.
And finally there's the crescendo of complete self absorption ignoring all the world,
When possibly more than insults, threats and of course inappropriate propositions will be hurled.

This is the joy of drinking throughout the night,
The journey that begins salubrious and ends somewhere out of sight.
No one can follow the exact pattern twice
Nor can you know exactly what will be the final price
Of the hurts and confusions that will organically arise
Which the brain will try to forget so the morrow may be replete with surprise.

I Know That You're Not Happy

I know that you're not happy with the way that we live
I've tried to do my best with all the things that I give
I don't want to be here baby living by myself
Put away and gathering dust up on a shelf
I know I haven't done the things I oughta do
The life I've made for us just isn't worthy of you
Can't you give me a chance to make another start
Let's try this all again before you tear us apart

I promise you're the most important part of my life
I've always been so proud with you now being my wife
From this day on you'll be a part of all that I do
I can't do this by myself baby I need you too
You still give me the shakes when you look over at me
Come and take my hand and let's see what we can be

It's Become Kind of A Contest

It's become kind of a contest —
Avoiding the traffic and making it across,
Before checking the paper to see who dropped away.
Then I go to get breakfast and start another day.
There's not a lot left for me,
Not many places that I want to see.
My kids have moved along and begun families of their own
And most of those back home I grew up with have already gone.

I'm not sure how much longer I can do this
But I'm still playing at the game.
I'll certainly try, calling everyone I know to prove that I'm still here.
There's less and less I can think of for me to finally miss
And I figure that everyone else looks at me and feels the same
So I'll keep playing by the rules until the day I quietly disappear.

I Guess I Wasn't Born To Invent

I guess I wasn't born to invent something useful —
Can't see me with an As Seen On TV gadget for sale.
The competition to produce such a thing is brutal
And the odds become tiny that one may prevail.

I know people are right now squeezing out ideas as fast as they can.
I can smell the burning of those brain cells as they ignite.
We'll soon have another singing fish panel from a very intense man
Whose energy is designed to insert his POV and to excite.

But I must have money because I'm born in this time and place
Where/when dollars are required in order to survive.
And I need to make myself jump into that race
So that I may find the wealth to keep myself alive.
Maybe I'm just weak behind the glasses with too much space between the ears
I should've been born when a man could succeed without the support of his
peers.

Your Love Has Removed Me

Your love has removed me from the world around.
My life has narrowed to the purpose of your view.
You are the source of all light and all sound.
I have focused myself upon the inspiration that is you.
What more is there for me to do or say
As long as you are happy with my acts?
I am here to follow your lead and not to stray —
To flow our way together and not to relax.

My world now is a much simpler place to be
Where distractions have been replaced by you.
Like the swimmer immersed within the eternal sea,
I move in the direction that your currents take me to.
Destiny then is met as time swings its hands
And what is to be ultimately crawls upon the sands.

Mice Upon The Chess Board

Mice upon the chess board
An ogre in the barn
A nightmare of disrepair
The end of peace and light

Disrupted and enchanted,
We have lost the way.
Order has been forgotten.
We shall pass within the night.

Hope has come to hopeless
And we'll not see the day.

Reality is lost through an unlocked gateway,
Cause and effect crushed beneath gravity's attack.
Nothing now seems to matter anyway
And there's no joy in looking back.

My Baptism Was A Simple One

My baptism was a simple one —
Part of the Sunday morning service.
Lots of people were already there
Since it didn't rain.

My wedding was well attended, I think —
I am not sure because I was kinda nervous.
But I think friends and family wanted to share
Because it didn't rain.

I expect my funeral will be sincere but short lived —
I guess my feelings about it don't serve a purpose.
Anyone may attend who might care
As long as it doesn't rain.

Baptism By Bridge

A different man came out of the water.
The one who entered was lost and alone.
The wet one who emerged was still alone
But no longer seeking a reason to matter.

VOLUME NINE

Love is a Goal

Love is a goal, a light in the distance,
That draws the lover past the muddy obstacles of apathy and lust.
To reach it finally without assistance,
To focus and move forward requires a journey of both faith and trust.
As you approach the loved one, excitement rises high.
Increasingly the brightness threatens to blind.
Breath is coming quickly and ultimately results in a sigh
And all that is becomes only what is in the lover's mind.

Of course, nothing can ever be as fine as it seems to be.
No one can live a life devoted to only one soul.
Distractions will undermine focus while trials will dull the view.
Your strength will ebb with the effort and routine will devastate you.
Much is required by life's tyranny upon the human heart.
Like a vacation fondly remembered, the search will be the finest part.

A Moment Now and Then

A moment now and then is as big as your life.
How do we prepare — how must we respond?
How is it fair to trip over an unseen opportunity
That suddenly rises up to change the course of what is happening
With an unexpected nor requested twist
That alters the sunny afternoon stroll
Into a serious hike through the darkening forest.
Gone are all certainties amid this descent into strife.

Once upon a time there was a great and immediate roar
But now there is only silence.
There was a frantic ear-bursting rush
That I thought would never end.
Then arrived the quiet
And I saw there was yet to be no more.

I Reckon I Drove

I reckon I drove in all four thousand miles or so —
West past the river, north to follow against its flow.
Then west again across plains that seemed tame with little to gratify
And then the dramatic gray wall of mountains that reached on past the sky.

I'd come from rolling hills and endless forests verdant and filled with history.
This all seemed less somehow and devoid of any sort of mystery.

I'd left my father with everyone else I'd ever known behind, growing smaller by the mile
With each and all of the disappointments and failures fading all the while.

I'd expected a new beginning a tabula rasa would give me the chance to make life right
And not to be haunted by the ghosts that had been created during the consequential night.

I've found since that life tends to follow a collective pattern, a path worn smooth across the ages.
You can attempt to skip ahead or run away but we're destined to live through all the pages.
I never see a face or stand in a place that I knew before
But they are all here with me — much a part of me — easily viewed through the always open door.

My Bow is Bent

My bow is bent and you are in my sight.
A clean shot at your heart is all I seek.
You are my prey, the purpose of the light.
You are the one, you the remarkably unique.

In you are the pleasures of this lifetime.
Your presence is a reward and a relief.
You rise above all upon the skyline
And fulfill the dedication of belief.

Let me be your hand, your shoulder, your comfort
And I will hide you beneath my wing.
You will need no one and nothing more to guarantee your support
And I will be sure that of what you need you will have everything.
Somehow I know you will learn to love me too
So I promise to guide you on your way through.

An Empty Page is a Scary Thing

An empty page is a scary thing like a bright light in an empty room
Which casts upon nothing where something would help define the place.
But here is the white blank space of the unknown and the yet to come.
Then the stark black type slowly spreading across its face
Begins to bring a thing which then defines and limits all abilities
And as such gives it form removing all other possibilities —
This is the beauty and the horror of it —
Where nothing is infinite something is most definite.

What is not can be anything perhaps something to love.
Once it is, opinions enter and try to decide its worth.
Unlikely it is to deserve praise as if it dropped from heaven above
Its angles will likely be compared to previous designs from out the earth.
Once begun each stroke removes a world of choices
Limiting what becomes to be decided by human voices.

There's Weird Shit Going On

There's weird shit going on out that way — I just don't believe I want to be
part of it —
Fucking weird shit that causes me to doubt the sanity
Of what's going on in that direction, that part of humanity.
I always turn the other way because that way ain't the way I want to be.
I don't feel like I belong there — they do not think like I do.
I don't have any idea what the difference is and it ain't something I'll
understand soon.
She called them deplorables and then lost her bid to lead us all.
Sometimes I'm just not sure about what we think or what's doing with these
party walls.

I grew up with bullies, took my knocks and gave them.
I just don't know any other way to act
Because what we are is what we've been and what we'll be.
I'm old but, like my daddy said, I still need a lot of learning and that's a fact
But I don't go out much anymore,
Though I've considered leaving this place altogether.

When It Was About To Happen

When it was about to happen,
I told her to hold on tight.
I never felt so close to anyone.
We seemed to melt simultaneously with delight.
Then we started uphill again,
Climbing slowly against the pull of the earth,
Feeling our weight exaggerated by the motion,
Eyes linked in a mutual devotion.

Until again the peak thrilled us with the imminent fall
And we screamed together as we pulled each other
Through the escalating descent of it all
With the alternating clinch and shudder.
And when we were through it, we did it again and again
Until we were worn out and so were at an end.

I Used To Watch Boris Karloff

I used to watch Boris Karloff movies where loved ones are brought back again,
Where love and science combine to return the loss that time did bring.
Lovelorn and Poe-etic the protagonist is maddened by the lonely vacuum,
Left to haunt his dreams within the confines of life's forlorn continuum.
Somehow the result of retrieving the fallen and the lost
Results in horror rather than a joyous return.
Trying to relive what has been has a cost
That provides the bringer a tragic lesson to learn.

I guess you are gone because you should be
Though I don't understand the movie we are in.
I would do anything to have you back with me
But I don't think I have the choice to retrieve what has been.
I would spend all my thoughts to have you here once more, you know,
But I believe now does not allow the return of long ago.

Hormones Are A Horror

Hormones are a horror in retrospect —
Like a toddler in diapers, the world is all for him.
For the victim of this drug, no desire is circumspect
And his acts produce results that are grim.
Hard to imagine why life requires such foolish drives
With arrogant and selfish notions reaching out to the world,
Where ego requires dominance of all — to only take and not to give
And displays of one way demeaning pleasure are ever hurled.

Some of us never learn to staunch this rush of fever.
We spend all our days rolling in the mud.
Some will become a more circumspect believer
And learn to follow a higher source than blood.
Wonder why we are led by such low tendencies
And so must overcome these base dependencies?

I Have A Dream Too

I have a dream too and it's always the same.
It is pervasive and it guides me on my way.
I don't have any other purpose — it tells me why I came.
Only this directs my steps through each and through every day.
You may not know me — you may not understand,
But I have been dreaming and I know you are the reason I am here.
I am just an actor in a universal story already planned.
I just follow direction and deal with opportunities as they appear.

I exist for you and am only to provide for your support.
I know you have lived without me until now
But look I'm here and my time is running short.
I need you to see me and then I'll be your answer to how.
Lean toward me in this right moment and say what you need
And we will find a way to move you forward just as it is decreed.

And Then It Was Over

And then it was over —
The lights were out,
The doors were locked,
And all the people drove away.

Silence loomed heavily
As the dry flies scratched steady at the heavy summer air,
As somehow the world kept spinning.
The sun and moon continued their sky crossing arc
And the seasons themselves never slowed at all.

But I was no longer there as before
And the world had returned to the pre-me life
Except for whatever good or damage I may have done.
Having drifted away like winter smoke,
Having left the city as well as the era,
I was gone and soon forgotten as the spinning never waned.

What Comes Comes

What comes comes
As it has forever been
And will always be.
That which we are yet to see
Will not answer why, any how, or when.

VOLUME TEN

Jesus Stands Quietly Alert

Jesus stands quietly alert
As if uncertain how to step in this pure new form
So like the old one, so dewy yet, as the darkness succumbs to light.

She, suspended in the shadows, awaits His first words
Near frantic to hear the explanation of this —
How He came to be again
What they were to do with this new awakening, this transcendence
Leaning forward, not daring to breathe
Not wanting to miss anything
Awaiting the answer to the why.

Then He spoke his first words to her in a voice hoarse with disuse in the cool
morning air —

Don't touch Me.
Go tell the boys I want to see them.
We'll meet in the city.

As she turned to go, Mary remembered nights before
When being cast aside had felt less of a shock.
Now sprinting away from the rising sun
Toward the still dark night,
She wondered.

What is Real

What is real
The echo of footsteps
The shadow of another
The vacuum of the universe that God once filled
The tingle that comes from acknowledgement
A warm breath that touches from I don't know where
And in the darkness all that is unseen and unsettling in its possibilities

The utterance of sound in air formed to draw another's gasp
Or symbols arranged upon a blank slate to stop the motion of those near

Chewing The Cud

Chewing the cud of a late summer morning
As the mist settles onto the grassy field,
I watch darkness recede and the warmth of another day become.

Here are possibilities and a whisper of joy is in the air.
Maybe you will arrive today and give purpose to my breath.
You are the body guarded.

I think of your face and I can't help but smile.
Yours is the life that makes living worthwhile.

My aimless plodding life seems unnecessary in this place
My actions don't bring nor prevent change under these spinning skies
I know only that you will make me matter here —
You're the one who can bring joy with those brilliant eyes

While I, an old man with sugar sprinkled across his pate,
Sit quiet until your presence is known — 'til then I wait.

Lightning Bugs

Lightning bugs dip and rise in the warm summer night
As the sun goes away
And we fade into the darkness
Losing sense of self.
We find our place just where we are —
No longer frantic with expectation and requirement
The only sound the sawing of unseen cricket legs hidden within the night.
So quiet the world now
Amid the regular suspiration of the trees.

We have seen the bright hot flame of the day
Endured its anxious pull drawing us into the spinning life
That ever taunts us with the open door ahead.
Such heat propelled us awkwardly twitching
Along an unseen path toward an unknown end
As such fuel silently evaporates shimmering and faint
And we begin to sense that a world exists outside after all
Only glimpsed before as we scrambled brain and brawn
Along and across as we were made to do.

Do Not Stop

Do not stop moving or your life will end
Ignore those haters who say you're too old
Stand up straight and swear you will never bend

Always come those who swear they are your friend
That you should listen to what you are told
Do not stop moving or your life will end.

Keep on going without a pause to mend
You will find yourself beginning to fold
Stand up straight and swear you will never bend

Those who love you will have their view to lend
They'll think your now gray life should be on hold
Do not stop moving or your life will end

Young strangers too will deign to condescend
Thinking their brief wisdom is manifold
Stand up straight and swear you will never bend

When life's light flickers, nothing to extend
As you stand at freedom's final threshold
Do not stop moving or your life will end
Stand up straight and swear you will never bend

Who Are You

Who are you — no don't tell me — I don't want to know.
Just keep looking at me the way you do
Like a hungry leopard ready for its next kill.
Don't stop looking at me — at least — not yet.

Just chew me up slowly starting at my mouth
And working whichever way you will.
Don't ask for permission or forgiveness
And don't stop until you've got all that you can get.

Don't miss the anticipated thrill —
Just keep chewing until everything gets still.

Go until you're done with me and this world is no more a part of who we are.
Your eyes drooping and your limbs gone numb with delight,
Sleep it off baby — your belly swollen with what I was —
Sleep until the day becomes the night.

Chew me eat me swallow me all.
Then I'll be gone but you'll still be here
As will the memory we made and left behind
For others to dream of and to strive to make again.

But why then do we need to make a memory
Lost in the grains as they fall away?
Can't we be a moment in all the time there is —
Then forgotten along with all the other moments
That are here for just today?

It Was A Virgin Land

It was a virgin land so lush they said that a squirrel could climb a pine tree in Carolina and reach the Pacific without touching the ground.

Then the civilized developers of the natural arrived and turned God's garden into their business.
The wonders given free to all became resources and the property of some.
The trees came down, the soil was turned, and the seemingly docile world was overcome —
Space eroded until now bodies are so tightly jammed together —

Closer together than the houses in Sherman Oaks
With the privacy of a homeless shelter —

So that today a squirrel can climb upon a man in Santa Monica and not touch ground until he reaches Myrtle Beach.

A Year Was Yanked Away

A year was yanked away — some hand waved unseen
And life as I knew it was no more

As I looked ahead, I couldn't imagine the horror would last more than another few weeks
Well maybe one more month

Okay then until summer is past
But there was no end, no sign of relief

And when I gave up and shrank my life to fit the world collapsed,
Well then of course it all came rushing back

So like life always is
This the episode seemingly unending which ended all the same.

I Ask Forgiveness

I ask forgiveness every day every day every day
And all of each night.
I feel the need to be forgiven —
To change the way I think and do —

Not to forget the hurts I've caused or those who cared for me that I left behind
But to create a life of compassion to stand against the ever spinning world
that never speaks at all.

This is what I need to do
Such is required to try to dampen the swell
So that I may see out toward the forever and not forget what I am to do.

But I have never been able to get off the beach
There's so much mushy sand in which to lie and the bonfire is so warm with
invitation
That I am forced to stay here and ignore the cold unknown hidden yet among
the trees.

I've Found Myself Alone

I've found myself alone again.
Now I don't know what I'm going to do.
This place is set up for couples, you see
And now once more there's only me.

I am as substantial as a shadow,
As noisy as the sunrise.
I can swirl my way like smoke among the starlings
And follow the light across the sky.

The world spins by so fast and constant.
The days go flying by.
I have to get out there and make a life of it.
Take a run and make a leap to board.
Catch up before it leaves me finally behind.

Everything I do, I think, is as it should be
And quite the thing to do
But no one ever notices and I go on alone.
Before I know it, everything I had is just gone.

Maybe you could take notice.
Maybe give me a chance to be myself
To show you I deserve some attention
To let me be the one you pull down from this lonely shelf.

The world spins by so fast and constant.
The days go flying by.
I have to get out there and make a life of it.
Take a run and make a leap to board.
Catch up before it leaves me finally behind.

I'm not forgiven, but forgotten.
Leave back the blame, there's nothing to recall.
No one can understand another.
We are doomed to know no one at all.

The world spins by so fast and constant.
The days go flying by.
I have to get out there and make a life of it.
Take a run and make a leap to board.
Catch up before it leaves me finally behind.

The Girls Blew Up

The girls blew up the morning before we had Mother's Day.
Their school exploded with them in it — two birds it was —
They were thriving which is not allowed.
They were learning which cannot be tolerated.

The school was made of blocks and primary colors.
The students wore comparable clothing.
Then it was all crumbles with dust and glass pieces flying.
The blast hole smelled of nitrate and fried beef.

People dug through the rubble for awhile.
Then they sat in the heat of the day with their heads down.
It looked like they were crying
But maybe they were relieved that it was over.

How much worse could it be now
Now that their daughters were no more?
How could there still be terror now?
Their dusty little boys could grow up to take an humble spouse.

Pieces of girl were all over —
Their brilliance scattered among the stars.
They were raised above these grubby young slayers
To shine forever down upon the world's continuing atrocity.

One More Breath

One more breath please to use to say I love you.
Thank you for the moment and the chance to say goodbye.
Now I can leave though I don't want to.
Since it's time to end this life, then I'll go quiet and you can just go.

VOLUME ELEVEN

It's Nearly Eight

It's nearly eight now. They'll be loading the car for school.
I would be telling them both to make a hundred.
I would maybe find her phone on the kitchen counter
And rush it out to her before she backed them all into the street.

I keep checking to see if she has called or left a message.
How could this have ended — how can I have just ceased to be?
This has been my life and now I'm not there
And yet the sun still rises and sets as if everything is the same.

And there are no messages no missed calls no emails.
I should stop checking and just move on.
I have certainly dreamed of less responsibility,
Of the freedom of no commitment.

But now there's a big hole where my heart was.
I never imagined that.
I reach out to care but no one is in sight
As I have lost all connection and float now alone.

Then it's dark and the kids will be getting ready for bed —
Dinner, a bath, a story, and tucked in.
I have always been a part of the process.
Now I sit quiet and without.

And the dreams will come soon —
Disjointed and lost horrors all —
And I will awaken, swing my arm in an arc across the bed,
Rediscovering the emptiness that lies with me.

The Bar

You weren't there last time but other girls almost as perfect
Agreed with a smile to talk with me at first sight.
And since time was still ticking and my confidence peaking
I had to go on without you through the night.

We were drinking and dreaming and dancing and daring
As we eased our way into the long dark together.
It started with losing ourselves in the swirling of the crowd.
Then found us getting louder with each succeeding round.
If you think you can love me then come on over here now.

A beer or two is what it takes to do it —
Take the corners off the hours and make them seem fine and right.
And as we were dancing with rhythmical glancing
We sailed together into the adventurous night.

Darkness and desiring, deliberately dashing
I've nothing more to say about what came after
But you're always invited and I'm endlessly excited
To be with you through the love and the laughter.

We were drinking and dreaming and dancing and daring
As we eased our way into the long dark together.
It started with losing ourselves in the swirling of the crowd.
Then found us getting louder with each succeeding round.
If you think you can love me then come on over here now.

Like the sour smell of beer mixed with the sweet scent of girls
I am part of the place now —taken for granted, I'm assumed.
As much as the bar and the dance floor I am here.
The guy you can drink and dance with all now presume.

We were drinking and dreaming and dancing and daring
As we eased our way into the long dark together.
It started with losing ourselves in the swirling of the crowd.
Then found us getting louder with each succeeding round.
If you think you can love me then come on over here and show me how.

You Release Me

You release me from the malady that rains upon my every day
The overarching gloom of responsibility from which there seemed no escape.
You cheer my heart and make me to feel that I matter after all
That what I say and what I think will be readily heard so I can celebrate.
I've been locked all my life inside a cold room tied and blindfolded nothing
to see or do.
You led me into a place I'd not seen before giving to me your light and warmth
To make a life that is worth the journey with your soft and giving self.
My focus is on you alone and all the wonders that you possess.

Eagerly the sun rises lighting bright the newborn day.
Morning brings the opportunities that were dreamed of in the night.
Ingenuous nature then breathes out the sweetness of the air
Like the green of the trees and the cool breezes of the world now.
You awaken and move gracefully on as I wonder,
Reaching out, how long before we are to be one.

Life in Perspective

We are the actors not the writers of these tales as they unwind.
We wander without guidance through the tunnels in our minds.
I've been looking for an answer as to why I'm here at all.
What I've found is your bright beauty and now I'm here with you to fall.

You are my purpose — she who stands among the sunflowers small and gray.
It's as if you have something you really need to say
But the photo only captures your dark eyes and silent hurt
As you are planted in the garden where you hide your secret heart.

I'm not ready for the graveyard as I look to move along
I'm still bathing in your beauty as it sparks another song.
The days I know are numbered just as the moments of our lives.
The end's around the corner because none of us survives.

Stay between the lines they say — don't move out of your own lane.
If we all just do what we're supposed to do, then we'll get through this
thing ok.
But what about the living of a life focused on a nightly dream.
Maybe then we could find some answers as we pick apart life's seams.

We are here until the lesson is learned or until it has been lost
Until time is over and we return to the river we have crossed and recrossed
Where another chance will be offered and we'll enjoy freedom once again
Out of time and without place back where we have always been.

I'm not ready for the graveyard as I look to move along.
I'm still bathing in your beauty as it sparks another song.
The days I know are numbered just as the moments of our lives.
The end's around the corner because none of us survives.

No fear or pain or dread with only grace to guide our way
With time to be as we are readied to begin another day.
Assured that troubles are not expected to go beyond this fright-filled place,
We return as another chapter begins and life once more ensues where a life
has been erased.

I'm not ready for the graveyard as I look to move along.
I'm still bathing in your beauty as it sparks another song.
The days I know are numbered just as the moments of our lives.
The end's around the corner because none of us survives.

Do You Want To?

Want to? want to? do you want to?
Want to? want to? do you want to?

Are you sure?
Do you really want to
Are you sure
Are you certain that you want to

Well then
Let's go
Let's go — do you want to
Want to want to do what you want to
just the way you want to — just you and me

Tell me show me to do what you want to
Like this just this way to do what you want to
Do you want to

Right now?
Are you certain
That you want to?

Just like this?
Should we do it
Do you want to
I'll make you happy
How is that
Ready again — already
So you want to?

Are you certain that you want to
Well then

If you really want to

Are you certain that you want to

Let's go
Let's go to do what you want to
Want to want to to do what you want to

Tell me show me that you want to
Like this just this way the way you want to
Do you want to

Right now?
Are you certain
If you want to, then let's go — you and me.

Toward Your Eyes

Now you've set sail again
And I'm moored here without again
How have I come back to this lonely darkening shore
Numbed by the hurt of loss within this watery space?

Maybe this will be the last time
Each course has seemed to be right
But along the way a sudden storm rises up to send me alee,
Then another course opens up
To take me toward another wish not glimpsed before

Here I am wishing that I were loosed upon the world
Like an arrow from its bow
As a cannon ball flies
Not going back again
Too fast to think it through
Headed straight now toward your eyes

False starts have been my life
I just don't know if I can leave this dock again
Each time I think I'm doing right — things are working as they should
And just before I've made it, I'm forced to abandon my way

Why does this happen to me?
What is there that I must do or say
To get to an end that is an end and to be what I need to be?
Maybe this time I'm too far out to sea

Maybe I always was
And just thought I was going straight along my quest
When I was only following along an endless line

Circling the vortex bent by the strain
That would pull me down some future unending day
Where I sink unnoticed into the dreaded inescapable drain

This puzzle is making me crazy
I'm a mouse that can't get to the cheese
Nothing more to say about my life
Except I've got to try again
This time with no hesitation
I'm to set a course straight toward your eyes

Have You Ever

Have you ever felt that

Holding her hand is about the most wondrous feeling there is
That her presence near is all you need to carry you over and around

Of all the good and bad and the choices that may be found
Nothing in this world matters more than this one

She's the answer to the unanswerable questions of your life now won
But even she cannot explain the ultimate reason why

If you had to spend the night apart you would surely die
So hold tight and never ever look away

Never ever look away

Little Lost One

Little lost one, scampering thoughtless through the garden greens, trying not to lose the rest.
Your father abandoned you, ignoring your love,
While your lonely mother so needed your friendship that she forgot
To take you aside and show you how to be.

Cat mama so empty within — devoid of spirit, finding warmth in other helpless, mindless, and feral unfallen
Who eating grains and meat by-products like yourself abandoned and without
Lack the knowledge that might bring consequence
Sniffing, squatting, and giving to all without discipline or the ability to choose.

Right and wrong the two faces upon the coin stare blankly back at you
You the giver giving indiscriminately without knowing you've a gift
Focused upon the helpless unherdable ones who cannot know they are lost already
Having been used and returned like the soiled cloth that is your lives.

For you raising your back slowly slithery seductively timed with your eyes for best effect
Nothing else past the moment exists.
Now smells of apple and the emptiness of innocence
Destined but stalled, ended but still walking, advancing but toward nothing, mewing quietly to no known purpose

Sunning again in the garden like yesterday and tomorrow without guard or direction.

No Place To Drive To

The faces I have kissed remain in the past.
No one is here with me now.
Time's going by faster than fast
And I just don't know how

To live each day giving love
To those who are already gone.
It was never quite enough
So now I'm here all alone.

The only key in my pocket is the one for my car.
From here on, it looks like I'll be on my own.
It doesn't really matter how near or how far.
I've no place to drive to called home.

I've seen tears and laughter.
I've given and I've got.
I don't know what comes after.
I gave it my one and only shot.

Near is the end of my story
And I'm already ready to go.
It all wasn't for anything like glory.
What it was for I don't yet think I know.

The only key in my pocket is the one for my car.
From here on, it looks like I'll be going on my own.
It doesn't really matter how near or how far.
I've no place to drive to called home.

I guess time will tell others
When I was right or did wrong
But the judgments are another's
So they'll write their own song.

Maybe after all I'm just a villain
Or maybe the one who made the way.
Hopes and dreams led me through it
While I did what seemed required by the day.

The only key in my pocket is the one for my car.
From here on, it looks like I'll be going on my own.
It doesn't really matter how near or how far.
I've no place to drive to called home.

Little Pigs

(Revised)

Little pig, little pig, let me come in.
You are the meal that I shall make tonight.
Open up now else I will destroy your house
Whether straw or stick or brick laid tight.

I'm knocking now upon your front door.
I hear you scurrying about like the others did before.
Your little hooded nails ticking skittish across the glassy floor.
It is the time to huff n puff
And blow the whole thing down — again.

Yes, I'm big and bad — I'm the big bad wolf,
The one your mother warned you about,
The one who is built to be hungry —
Ready to eat you up and then to spit you out.

I am the wolf.

You may turn the key to hide your selfish face
But I will be just outside trampling through the flower bed,
Inhaling all of the light and all of the air — I am bred
To work a squall upon your place.

Your chubby little self cannot escape my pursuit.
Zaftig sweet and rosebud soft you're the one that I want
To chew and savor, dripping unctuous from the spit.
Give it up — not enough bricks in the world for you to flaunt.

Yes, I'm big and bad — I'm the big bad wolf
The one your mother warned you about

The one who is built to be hungry —
Ready to eat you up and then to spit you out.

I am the wolf, the one you've been waiting for.

You can crouch behind or beneath — depending on how tight you've stretched
your piggy skin.
Walls can't stop me nor even dull my blast.
Start your praying, your screaming — you can plead with me or you can ask.
I'll still devour the whole of your chinny chin chin.

Build your house as big as you might
Rig up security with bright flashing lights
I'm coming with lungs filled to blow you down and away
And bring the end to your worthless string of days.

Yes, I'm big and bad — I'm the big bad wolf
The one your mother warned you about
The one who is built to be hungry —
Ready to eat you up and then to spit you out.

I am the wolf, the one you've dreaded,
The one that twitches your little piggy snout.

It has always been this way just before the end.
You've sat to feast at the old folks' ease,
Fattened your butt, buttered your little cakes, and sweetened your tea
And after all this when I knock on your door your aim is to flee.

But you knew I was coming, as sure as the night.
You knew that nothing could stop me
So why did you turn your back to the light
And why do you call me evil when my cause is so easy to see?

I'm knocking now upon your front door.
I hear you scurrying about like the others did before.
Your little hooded nails ticking skittish across the glassy floor.

It is the time to huff n puff
And blow the whole thing down — again.

Yes, I'm big and bad — I'm the big bad wolf,
The one your mother warned you about,
The one who is built to be hungry —
Ready to eat you up and then to spit you out.

I am the wolf.

What Happened

What happened on this day in ...
1951 a child was born to an unwed mother who gave him away as soon as
she could
1819 John Keats announced the arrival of "To Autumn" with its mellow
fruitfulness
I know that soft-dying day as much as I'd like to forget it and would
Rather than add another bow to the history that's soon to be my life
Years that have already passed many times over and consciously stood
Which of those repetitious yet to be announced days will be on my tombstone
Which will mark the end of what I can do and say for ill or for good.

I feel as if night is here and forever will be
I see no light in the distance to fortify me
Only the cool of the dry and silent tomb
Dusty bones lying still within the room
All light and laughter gone forever more
As what was I has now exited the always open door.

He is a Killer

He is a killer — a murderer of truth —
A disseminator of lies and harsh judgment.
Best to ignore the madness, to move on with the peace of the world
Nothing will be here tomorrow regardless
So live your life facing the light.

VOLUME TWELVE

The Why

She was blonde and blue-eyed
Tiny and smart too.
We had the world to talk about
Between the kisses and the hugging
After the holding and the touching.

Then her mom would come walking through the living room.

Not a word nor a notice
Just a ship plowing through the night —
Then she'd sail back again later
While we'd look up like chickens in the pen.

It turned out her daughter knew the reason —
Her mom had a bottle in the garage.
She wouldn't talk about drinking
But she'd sneak a walk through the house
Until sleep took her over and she could get through the night.

So we'd have to move to my place
Upstairs in a little corner house
Right by the main road where the big trucks
Roared cacophonous through the dark

Not quite the same, as the walls kept us private,
While we might jointly discourse upon the values of Locke.

These years later I'm a driver going somewhere nightly
And she's a housewife and mother elsewhere down the road.
I don't know if she's found need yet for the garage bottle
But I understand when a numbing of past dreams might be required.

It's The Night Before

It's the night before and the stars shine starkly bright
Then fade one by one into nothing as the sky turns steady into light
Tears are a bloody and a conquering river rife
Flowing through toward the imminent end of my life

I know I shall not see another sunset
No more my followers nor my queen
Living is never guaranteed yet
The end tomorrow will be an awe-filled bloody scene

It is to be the final battle
The one that has often been foretold
Spears will shake and armor will rattle
The weak will cower before the bold

I will stand unsheathed, alone, and ready
And judgment will be handed down
Please God help me to steady
And hand freely over my care-worn crown

Goodbye to those who stayed with me
I know you expected to find a better end
To hell with those who set my weary life free
I'll not look back toward either foe or friend.

Not to curse the one who walked away
Though I have still to understand the reason why
Not to praise all those who loved and stayed
No judgments are mine now only time to die.

The journey has been a hard one
As it must be for each and for all
And I believe I have lost no more than I've won
As I approach this final and fatal fall

Now is the time to add accounts for each to see what he's left
I'll not be here to justify your selves not here to judge your heft
Find your reason for continuing, your striving to be
And, until your doorway is open, find your own way to see to see.

It's The 3am Wake Up

It's the 3am wakeup call that my body set just for me
When a merciless tic of my mind drags me up from the solace of sleep
Screaming and kicking helpless all along the jagged way
To this the darkest of the dark from which everything has been swept
Darker than light has ever been light even at the bustling noon of my days
More alone than ever alone in this empty and solitary place
Where I am to face the remainder of what is the night

To learn what only is like.
To feel the cold that lives at the end my way.

It's The Summer Solstice Again

It's the summer solstice again, the brightest day of the year
When the world leans as close as it can toward the warmth of the enchanted sun
Spinning in concert with eternity, completing its journey from darkness into light

It's Midsummer again with only the briefest of the night
Now filled with comedy magic and the shadowy forest mists
Where love's potion misplaced still may not thwart love cast haphazard upon the shore

Here passion may its true aim find though masquerading lions roar
Today the sun completes its climbing of its ladder into Cancer before its declination
Here to create an ultimate climax, a thrill to know regardless of perilous flight

This the time of temporary joy surrounded by dreamlike love and sudden delight
Where mystic magic and abrupt translation may swirl about our dazzled heads
And we may determine that there is a way to move back from violet into white

As we travel steady each day now toward the increasing night
With what we gain today to aid us in our justifiably growing fright.

Come And Be With Me

It's been a long hard day
And the night is coming fast
Come get me now and say to me
I can be finished and you will make the way

Come and be with me
Make me the one you want
Don't ever leave me please
Make me what you need me to be

I don't think I can get there
I don't think that I can
I don't want to be left there
I can't be that man

I'm at the brink of going
I won't be running on through the night
I'm at the brink of knowing
I need you to take me on into the light

Baby, I need you with me tonight
We'll be in our glory only when you're here
Lifting us toward the heights above the rest
Giving us a life that together will be blessed

I don't think I can get there
I don't think that I can
I don't want to be left there
I can't be that man

My words are meant to call to you
I need you to listen close

Nothing's right without you now
I'm the thorn while you're the rose

You are my epiphany
The life that lights the world
Please now come with me
And we'll be forever curled

I don't think I can get there
I don't think that I can
I don't want to be left there
I can't be that man

Why Do You Hate Me

For years, we've been one together
Even before we were we were
We've looked long into each other's eyes
We've watched the world in its constant spinning
But now you've taken me by surprise

You won't say that you don't love me
But you won't tell me the truth
You just told me to get out of there
Now I'm in a car driving nowhere
With all that I own piled up to the roof

How could this have happened
Why do you hate me suddenly
How long has this been coming
All I can feel is the sudden heat

Why do you hate me
What is it I've done
How can you think of me
With such frustration in your tone

I was there for you when the day turned to night
I held your hand and told you ok
You told me that I was your guiding light
But that's not what you told me today.

I don't want to fight with you
I haven't won one yet
I'd rather just walk away from you
And find a way to take what I can get

I treated you then and always as a lady
I thought that you deserved my care
Maybe you preferred to be shoved in the dirt
Maybe I should have pushed my way until you hurt

Maybe respect only counts in friendship
Maybe lovers need to fight and forget
Maybe a steady path isn't romantic
Maybe mine is still not settled yet

Why do you hate me
What is it I've done
How can you think of me
With such frustration in your tone

I don't want to fight with you
I haven't won one yet
I'd rather just walk away from you
And find a way to take what I can get

I've learned that tall, dark, and gruesome turns on all the lights
Nothing short of a challenge provides the dips and peaks of delight
Kind and gentle is ok to start but only goes so far
Bullies rule and so comfort is then eaten by desire

The excitement of the cowboy — the danger of the jock
Nothing slow and steady — there's no telling where it'll stop
Don't hold too tight — don't expect anything beyond the now
Promises are forgotten nothing lasts here anyhow.

Why do you hate me
What is it I've done
How can you think of me
With such frustration in your tone

I don't want to fight with you
I haven't won one yet

I'd rather just walk away from you
And find a way to take what I can get

You've taught me better for next time
I won't expect a night to last
I'll move first and that'll be fine
And I'll just forget the past.

I May Not Be

I may not be a part of your life anymore
But I'm not done with mine just yet
I have my purpose and I'm swinging hard as long as I can go
Never finished until I'm finished, I'll not stop until the final horn does blow.

You can drive your glossy little red car
To have your nails shined and to add color to your hair
You may pet your sycophantic mewling multicats
And have your succups over to lounge within your trendy lair

You can spend your time with the latest styles
Reading bestsellers while decked out to the nines
But nothing you do will last beyond the final breath you take
While my words will remain long past your gently scented wake.

Don't speak to me — don't mention my name
Nothing more is needed from you on my behalf
I've come here now to call you out with all those who seek their seasonal fame
As your hard glare skips like a tiny stone across my mirrored lake

I in jeans and tee was never right among your crowd
Who are all light and surface while describing the flaws of the world out loud
I not calculated enough when my turn occasionally comes
I never knew how to gauge the breeze stirred by all those perfectly patterned
tongues

Leave me to my doing — I'll do what's still to be
I'll spend my nights pursuing the just right word to fit
You're the one with dreams of grandeur — a maven on a spree
While I just couldn't find a way to really give a shit.

All those smiles and all the posing quests
Gracious among your carefully chosen guests
Sipping and grazing with those just like you never opposing
Obsequious, shallow, and pitiless pandering flits

Always just the right expression
Always the word to move the night along
Your mouth a sweet digression
Willing to ignore the right or to praise the wrong

I'd find a way to punish you but there are laws that go against it
You take up space without justifying the cost
I wasn't sure for awhile but now I've sensed it
I was entranced at first but now I am no longer lost.

And finally, this is all for you the milquetoast moral warrior blind to virtue
As well as the fearless fashion critic labeled and stunningly donned
With words designed to please the invited listener
And a smile to hide any adherence to what's really real.

Tonight

Before a mirror with no reflection
Two sallow bodies blooded but worn
Left with no further conviction
Silently dreading what is yet to be born

Slender and pale
Tonight we will wander an inescapable maze
With no recourse or direction
All life's ambitions will suddenly and finally blaze

Lead me to your bedside
Bring all your anticipation and hope
Await what happens in the darkness
No no no no no no no no no no
No no no no no no no no no no
No no no no no no no no no no

There is no tomorrow
Only continuing darkness — nothing more to be
Lay back — you've naught to say here
You're lost among the shadows — there is nothing more to see

There was a yesterday
When the sun shown bright and clearly near
When destiny offered direction and purpose
And joy seemed always to be nearly here

Those days have been lost for us now
We've lived beyond our lives' intent

What remains is dark and dangerously solemn
No no no no no no no no no no
No no no no no no no no no no
No no no no no no no no no no

Slumped and bedraggled we will soon not be.

My Sister Stopped By Family Planning

My sister stopped by family planning because she was sick in the mornings
So they gave her the cure for a price and then she ran off to Charlotte
Where I hope she feels better but is lost no doubt within that swirling crowd.

I am not permitted to discuss her illness with the neighbors
Who might consider less of our family since she wasis a good girl
And so to avoid confrontation we do not think of her out loud.

What is it about nerve endings that overwhelm a moral code —
A little tickle distracts from reason, subsumes thought, focuses on the moment.

Why are the arms of another more important than your own regard —
A need to destroy loneliness and to be allowed to look for awhile into those
eyes.

How can a new found pleasure change the rest of how you will be —
As past and future dissolve into now and no thing else matters

Had her name been Mary, we could have claimed a holy cause
But since there will be no child born to help us we are left with no because.

You Never Knew Me

Why won't I listen to every word you say
Why do I study the turning of the sky
Rather than the lines that make your face
Why do I avoid eye contact with your smiling friends
Why do I come and go as I do in a state of only me

You are part of a social always-smiling world that does for itself
While I cannot see beyond the blue tarp along the street
And the newly dug brown hole in the churchyard — so deep so dark so cold
I do not find warmth in your dinner parties nor hope in your daily routine

You never knew me — you never wanted to
You took my offered hand and showed me to your world
And said what's mine is yours — come be with me
But never took the time to understand — I can't do that.

I am sorry I do not meet your needs
That I do not dress the way you think I should
I can never overlook how this world continues to bleed
I cannot get over it and I never could.

Your guests are dressed and showered
They know just what to do and say
They smell just like the flowers
That bloom out in your garden
Through each long sunny summer day

Your nails are brightly polished
Your hair's a perfect shape
I guess my jeans and t-shirt
Do not fit in your landscape

You never knew me — you never wanted to
You took my offered hand and showed me to your world
And said what's mine is yours — come be with me
But never took the time to understand — I can't do that.

The kids will have to choose now
To decide who they should believe
Are you the shallow selfish bitch I ran from
Or am I the puzzled loser who chose you to deceive.

No two persons were ever more different
We were the answer to only but nothing else
Of course if we had not been each so lonely
Those kids would have never had a pulse.

You never knew me, you never really cared
You wanted to defeat only at any cost required
You never knew me, you never even cared
You — it as all about you — you alone conspired

You never knew me — you never wanted to
You took my offered hand and showed me to your world
And said what's mine is yours — come be with me
But never took the time to understand — I can't do that.

I've Lived Through Numerous Popes and Presidents

I've lived through numerous Popes and Presidents.
I've watched my friends and kin fall silently away.
I don't want to discuss it — I'm not something out of history.
But I do what I ever could as easy as I ever should.
That's my story
That's my story
That's my story up 'til today.

The kids I went to school with, played ball and kissed at parties with
Have gotten old and gone away — those still standing must think I'm a myth
Always moving, never stopping
A stalwart stinkin' monolith — how's he doing that?
Why's he doing that?
I wish he'd just shut up
And be done with it.

Too much going — so many words — don't add to the congestion
Move on down to the duck pond or just go play with your grandkids.
Let the world spin quiet for awhile and let somebody else have a turn
Your time had a now but has since spun away.
That's my story
That's my story
That's my story up 'til today.

But I can't lay down yet because you're still out there yet
You the unfulfilled dream that haunts my dreary sleep
Maybe you'd like to come to me and we could be then ever we.
That can be my dream now — let's make it real somehow.

Come on here
Come on to me.
Let's together see.

Every day is Sunday now — the sky is always bright.
I'm to show those watching just how to make a life end right.
But you could help me — bring your self and bring your self to say.
Don't ever stop don't let me stop
And hold my hand while we dance our time away.
Come on here
Come on to me.
Let's together see.

There are songs yet to be born — adventures still to be.
Let's not be less than we can.
Yes I'll admit I'm old but I ain't dead yet.

There are Things I Can Do

There are things I can do and things I cannot
Things I want and things I avoid
Not much out there for me yet to see
I believe I'll ignore it all and just try to be.

I have gone past the arc of age
And can only see back to the high point near behind.
What happened before is no longer mine
To remember or regret.

VOLUME THIRTEEN

Here We are at Last

Here we are at last in the same plane again
As time and space have mutually converged.
Although we have been spinning in different orbits,
Today we two bright stars have finally and noisily merged.

In the resultant quiet, I can sense the drizzled rain
Dropping between the sheltering trees —
Its cadence like a slowly romantic ballad
That with its soothing presence cools the sympathetic breeze.

In this long anticipated evening your face is all I see.
You are the reason I still find my fated way.
Let's hold hands and walk ourselves together
Toward the end of each remaining kind and perfect day.

You are the one I was born to be with —
You the perfect soul that I must agree with.

The Stray

The neighborhood stray mews near your front door.
Then you gently set a bowl of milk just outside his reach
So as not to frighten him away.

The golden finches and the shadowy wrens twitter past your curtains
Swirling and alighting around your hanging feeders
That sway beneath their weight.

The plate by the back door is scrubbed to shiny
By whatever critters gnawed the supper's remains
During the silent searching of last night.

The grandsons adopted from incapable parents
Gather by you to hear a children's tale
Of danger and rescue in the frightening woods.

I sit on the sidewalk in the summer sun being dispossessed
Wondering what next indignity will come to me and to the rest.

Dying in America

We live in a world where the rising tide of life spills over.
Swarms of needy appear to see what you can do
But it's hard to focus on the many — maybe you can help the ragged few
As others are stepping into and tripping upon one another
Scattered across the hard blank dusty streets.
They live tarped, inert, and within their own small points of view —
Give me money and I'll buy food — any moment this could as well be you
And the world goes around and around and around.

As the unlucky are overwhelmed by the flood, so the successive lost must live without.
You can't save them all while you're trying to save yourself.
We're all drowning within the ironic loneliness of the selfish mass.
One for one and all for me — watching as failure silently pulls us away,
Swept down and out of sight by the struggle.
Now there's only isolation within the madness that surrounds
And yet the world goes around and around and around.

Love for everyone is out there someplace and finding it should be the goal
As imminent loss chases with its deadly hissing blade just above and behind us all.
When dodging the fatal cut and without time to waste,
Do what you can while the daylight lasts.
Paddle straight toward anyone you have and live in the moment that you're given
Don't go out there wandering aimless as the hard times go down.
Still you know the world will continue to go around and around and around.

The "Get Me Out of Here" Blues

I had a friend who I used to drink with
And a girl that would give me a smile
He and I would go to the fights some
She would kiss me at night for awhile

But somehow they wound up drinking together
They didn't bother to tell me so
But they went from hard drinks to sweet kisses
And now they're mister and missus
And its just time now for me to go

I'm stuck in this place with nothing to do
No one is left here that I want to know
Just give me a minute to hunt for my shoes
I just got those "Get me out of here" blues

I had a batch of kids who all loved me
Who needed me to help them to start
I tried to show them right from wrong,
I helped them figure out their part

But now they've grown up and moved on
They don't have time to listen to my plan
Got their own families to guide and support
Can't think about my life getting short.
So they just do as much as they can.

I've been stuck in this place with nothing to do
No one is left here that I want to know
Just give me a minute to hunt for my shoes
I just got those "Get me out of here" blues

I have no fire to warm me
No one to hold at night
I guess that's the end of my story
So I'll get my self on out of sight.

Don't worry about or pity me
I'm not a one to moan
I'll go and do because it's time
And then yours will come and so on.

Oh Lord I knew this was coming someday
But I never knew what to do
So I guess I'll soon be on my way
I hope the one I'll be seeing is you

I've been stuck in this place with nowhere to go
No one is left here that I want to know
Just give me a minute to hunt for my shoes
I just got those "Get me out of here" blues

Goodbye Now

My day is done now
No use pretending
What's done is done
There's no happy ending

I'll try to smile on
Though my time is over
No one can make a difference
But I'll always love her

The sun will rise tomorrow
By then I will be gone
No more worries, no more sorrow
Only right — no more wrong

I will always love her
And I hope she will remember me
So that when time comes around
She'll know that we are again to be

Dreams don't really die
But they may be delayed some
No one knows better than I
The joy that yet may come

Goodbye for now then
Please don't forget me
There will be a time when
We'll be what we're supposed to be.

More Than An Itch

The girls are all licking bananas
The boys' jaws drop in return
There is laughter in amazement
Before the moaning begins its slow burn

It's more than an itch my darling
It's the gear that drives each life
With desire comes the need for holding
And completion overwhelms daily strife

All five contribute to the effort
As the outside world falls away
No one can escape their body
But our needs come together for love's day

It may be our souls are most important
They can raise us above the curse of life
But it's the nerve endings of our bodies
That will gift us a husband or a wife

You Just Can't Stop

You just can't stop, can you?
You have to keep pushing on this unfinished man
With your never-ending list of instructions.
I said I was sorry, hung my head, shuffled my feet
While you rewound and started it all again.

Well I know I did wrong dear
And probably will do it some more
So let's just admit we're done here
And you can continue your search for
That impeccable — that indefectible — that immaculate man

We started out ignoring the differences
Focused on gracefully addressing each need
Tip toeing past that which could never meet
You going ever west while I was stumbling south
Unable to imagine what would be expected of me

I guess you realize now that I just can't be fixed
That I might be a problem right down to my foundation
Not all your directions and all your explanations
Will make much of a difference
No, they are never ever going to be enough.

Well I know I did wrong dear
And probably will do it some more
So let's just admit we're done here
And you can continue your search for
That impeccable — that indefectible — that immaculate man

By the way when you find that guy
And I surely hope you will do it
I want you to look into his perfect eyes
And heave at him all the shit you threw at — me.

Well I know I did wrong dear
And probably will do it some more
So let's just admit we're done here
And you can continue your search for
That impeccable — that indefectible — that immaculate man

I Dreamed Of You

I dreamed of you last night as the darkness led me away.
You spoke softly and reached out to me so gently —
It was as if we'd never argued and you were here to stay.
We were together again in the brilliant light of dreaming.

You smiled as did everyone — no tears, no shouting between us.
You kissed me too just as you did so often before.
There were no memories of hardship or of loss
As we strolled hand in hand through the peaceful light of dreaming.

A tiny one was here amid the many smiles on this day —
A little girl who looked up and called me daddy.
She tried but could not keep her excitement contained
While we walked beneath the perfect light of dreaming.

Holding your hands made me to smile as well.
I wanted never to leave this place of love so good and right.
Such joy was all around with only a happy future to foretell
So to always be together in the clear pure light of dreaming.

But I knew when I arose in the cold and cheerless night
That what I saw in that heavenly place could not ever be again
That you and all I love have long been taken from my sight
And when I wake all that will remain is the searing light of dreaming.

The Billions Flow

The billions flow toward apogee and perigee
While cancer claims another life summarily.

Tumors hurt like the devil no matter which way you lean.
With such impending terrors, flying away is not the thing.

G Force rises as we speed away from earth
Into the realm of space.
Can we withstand the pressure
Of the ever fastening pace?

Mars — war itself — beckons with its flirtatious red light
While a young mother's damaged heart gives up its fight.

Even billions are not a blanket to cover all —
We still have to decide who will rise and who will fall.

Can you fly into zero gravity?
Can you jump up to the moon?
Will you live to see your grandkids grow?
Such decisions will be needed soon.

Hunger and homelessness should be considered first
Before launching into darkness to please a rich man's thirst.

I hope that none of the rich men develop a glioblastoma
Because I doubt even they can successfully blast off in a coma.

I Heard

I heard ya'll wrote me off awhile ago
And decided it's time for me to say good night.
Bless your heart, I want ya'll to know
That at this moment I'm still upright.

I reckon that the Lord above
Is the only one to guide us through.
I'm dependent upon His ever present love —
Not sure how He feels right now about you.

When the time is right for me to go,
Let's pull the plug no need for lots of thinking.
There'll be no regrets for me you know.
I won't run around like a headless chicken.

Since the end might could come any time now,
I guess we should agree and not fight.
Just remember that until the final snow
I intend to be here still upright.

M — I Know You

I know you haven't been here for long
But the thought of you has

It has buoyed me over and beyond the dry and pain filled years
Of loneliness that sat upon me like a granite slab
Squeezing the air and life out and crippling my need to fly to you

We all lose in the end
I'd just like to have you near to me
To be with me as life offers up
Its surprises in the moment

Could you just be my friend
Just stay close for awhile

You don't have to love me unless you want to
You can do what you want as often as you will
Please let me into your world
Maybe we could spend some time together
And help each other climb those hills

Please let me into your world
and we will part the darkness with our light

Yes

Yes I get depressed
Then I get up and I get dressed
I am occasionally impressed
But mostly I must confess
I am generally not ok

Printed in the United States
by Baker & Taylor Publisher Services